THE E-MYTH
REVISITED

Also by
MICHAEL E. GERBER

E-Myth Mastery

The E-Myth Manager

The E-Myth Contractor

The E-Myth Physician

The E-Myth
Revisited

*Why Most Small Businesses
Don't Work and
What to Do About It*

MICHAEL E. GERBER

 HarperBusiness
An Imprint of HarperCollins*Publishers*

HarperCollins books may be purchased for educational, business, or sales promotional use. For information please write: Special Markets Department, HarperCollins Publishers, Inc., 10 East 53rd Street, New York, NY 10022.

THIRD EDITION

Library of Congress Cataloging-in-Publication Data

Gerber, Michael E.
   The E-myth revisited: why most small businesses don't work and what to do about it / Michael E. Gerber. — 1st ed.
     p. cm.
   ISBN 0-88730-728-0
   1. Small business—Management. 2. Entrepreneurship. 3. Success in business. I. Title.
HD62.7.G458 1995
658.02'2—dc20   94-46667

---

04 05 06 07 08 ❖/RRD 65 66 67 68 69 70

To My Father,

I wish he were here.

CONTENTS

ACKNOWLEDGMENTS

I would like to express my deepest gratitude to the many people with whom I've worked to produce the ideas that are presented in this book, as well as for the support needed to complete it.

To Ilene Gerber, my wife, partner, and editor, without whose intensity of purpose, dedication to the truth, and love for the work, both in our business and in the rest of the life we share together, neither this book, our business, nor our marriage would have been possible.

To Shana, Kim, Hillary, Sam, and Alex Olivia, my children, who have given to me more than they have received, in ways only a father can truly know.

To all my associates at E-Myth Worldwide, present and past, whose commitment to the ideas in this book, as well as to each other and our clients, have given meaning to the words by living them, even when it was impossible and when there seemed to be no good reason for doing so.

To all our thousands of clients over the years who have put their trust in our integrity, and, in the process, taught us at least as much as we taught them about what it means to transcend scarcity with excellence.

To Nancy and Bob Dreyfus, my sister-in-law and brother-in-law, whose wisdom, love, and generous spirits have touched me more than they can possibly know.

To Virginia Smith at HarperBusiness, whose caring, intelligent friendship has seen me through the most dismal moments of writing with a gentle, open, and willing nature that enabled me to be myself in the moments I least wanted to be, without apology or explanation.

And, finally, to all my readers who continue to support my work so enthusiastically.

Thank you all.

FOREWORD

It has been fifteen years since *The E-Myth* was first published. In my case, fifteen full years. A lot has happened in the interim—with my family, my business, my life. Many wonderful things, many good things, many painful things. And, if it's true what Don Juan said in *Tales of Power*, that "The basic difference between an ordinary man and a warrior is that a warrior takes everything as a challenge while an ordinary man takes everything either as a blessing or a curse," then I am as guilty of being an ordinary man as the next guy, and, on occasion, have ascended to the warrior state when God saw fit to provide me with the power.

In these fifteen years, I have experienced near financial and business disaster as well as incredible victories; have built a 16-year marriage into an exquisite partnership with my wife, Ilene; have become the father of two extraordinary children, Sam and Alex Olivia (the total is now five, ages nine years to thirty-eight years); have entered the anointed state of grandfatherhood thanks to my daughter Kim and my son-in-law John, who have blessed us with

Sarah, Elijah, Noah, Hannah, and Isaiah; have traveled throughout the world speaking to hundreds of thousands of small business owners in Australia, Canada, Spain, New Zealand, Japan, Puerto Rico, Mexico, Indonesia, and, of course, in almost every major city in the United States. And, through it all, I have been the grateful recipient of unrestrained support and caring from many of those whose lives I have in some way managed to touch and whose paths I have crossed.

In short, the years have been exhilarating, challenging, frustrating, exhausting, debilitating, boring, enlightening, rewarding, and, after all is said and done, a handful for anyone, especially for a guy my age with a penchant for going to the wall without concern for the damage I do to the leading parts of my body.

This book, then, is a product of the last fifteen years, as well as a product of the fifteen years that preceded them. It was almost exactly eight years before *The E-Myth* was published that I founded our company, E-Myth Worldwide, which has provided the fuel and experience for the point of view I have shared with those of you who have read *The E-Myth*, and with those of you who are about to read this book.

In the years since *The E-Myth* was published, many of my readers—as well as many of our small business clients—have asked me to clarify specific aspects of *The E-Myth* point of view so they could better apply it to their businesses. This book answers many questions that *The E-Myth* has raised over the years, offering both new and previous readers the opportunity to approach their businesses with renewed vigor and a sharpened mindset through an expanded experience of *The E-Myth* principles.

Toward that end, I have attempted to answer the most important questions I have been asked about the principles covered in each chapter by means of a running dialogue with a wonderful woman named Sarah (not her real name) with whom I've spent quite a bit of time over the past year. Sarah's experience in business, her patience, intelligence, and passion have helped me to address the challenging issues of our small business clients in the reorganization of their minds as well as their businesses. It is in response to Sarah's frustrations, and her very personal inquiry, that I have endeavored to clarify for the reader the E-Myth Point of View. I hope that Sarah and her questions are as engaging to you as they have been to me.

But, before I introduce you to Sarah, I'd like to share with you some thoughts about small businesses and the people who own them.

The question has often been asked of me, "What do the owners of extraordinary businesses know that the rest don't?"

Contrary to popular belief, my experience has shown me that the people who are exceptionally good in business aren't so because of what they know but because of their *insatiable need to know more.*

The problem with most failing businesses I've encountered is not that their owners don't know enough about finance, marketing, management, and operations—they don't, but those things are easy enough to learn—but that they spend their time and energy defending what they think they know. The greatest businesspeople I've met are determined to get it right no matter what the cost.

And by getting it right, I'm not just talking about the business.

I mean that there is something uplifting, some vision, some higher end in sight that "getting it right" would serve.

An ethical certainty, a moral principle, a universal truth.

Which is not to say that those I'm inclined to think of as extraordinary would necessarily communicate it that way. Many can't. Even if they had the inclination, they simply don't have the words for it. But it's still there all the same. You can see it in their eyes, feel it radiating from their bodies, hear it in the timbre of their voices.

On the other hand, notwithstanding the search for "something higher," the best of the best I have known are extraordinarily grounded people; they are compulsive about detail, pragmatic, down-to-earth, in touch with the seamy reality of ordinary life. They know that a business doesn't miss the mark by failing to achieve greatness in some lofty, principled way, but in the stuff that goes on in every nook and cranny of the business— on the telephone, between the customer and a salesperson, on the shipping dock, at the cash register.

And so the great ones I have known seem to possess an intuitive understanding that the only way to reach something higher is to focus their attention on the multitude of seemingly insignificant, unimportant, and boring things that make up every business. (And that make up every life, for that matter!)

Those mundane and tedious little things that, when done exactly right, with the right kind of attention and intention, form in their aggregate a distinctive essence, an evanescent quality that distinguishes every great business you've ever done business with from its more mediocre counterparts whose owners are satisfied to simply get through the day.

Yes, the simple truth about the greatest business-people I have known is that they have a genuine fascination for the truly astonishing impact little things done exactly right can have on the world.

It is to that fascination that this book is dedicated.

This book is a guide for those who see the development of an extraordinary business as a never-ending inquiry, an ongoing investigation, an active engagement with a world of forces, within us and without, that continually amaze and confound the true seekers among us with awesome variety, unending surprises, and untold complexity.

While it may seem obvious, this fascination with the development of an extraordinary business is not the same as a fascination with success.

Certainly not the success we normally think of. Some end point which, having reached it, enables one to say, "I did it!" Because my experience has taught me only too well that end points in the development of an extraordinary business are instantly replaced by beginning points.

So, this book is not about endings, but about beginnings, about the never-ending game, the delightful and exhilarating process, the continuous evolution of our senses, of our consciousness—of our humanness—which only comes from being present in the moment, from being attentive to what's going on.

I believe that our business can provide us with a mirror to see ourselves as we are, to see what we truly know and what we don't know, to see ourselves honestly, directly, and immediately.

I believe that our business can become an exciting metaphor for "The Way."

A wise person once said, "Know thyself." To that honorable dictum I can only add for the businessperson on the path of discovery, good traveling and good luck.

I might also add a few instructive words from another wise man, Anthony Greenbank, who said in *The Book of Survival*, "To live through an impossible situation, you don't need the reflexes of a Grand Prix driver, the muscles of a Hercules, the mind of an Einstein. You simply need to know what to do."

Good reading.

Michael E. Gerber
Santa Rosa, California
June, 2001

INTRODUCTION

I think that maybe inside any business, there is someone slowly going crazy.

Joseph Heller
Something Happened

If you own a small business, or if you want to own a
small business, this book was written for you.

It represents many thousands of hours of work we have
done at E-Myth Worldwide over the past twenty-four
years.

It illustrates a belief, created and supported by the
experiences we have had with the thousands of small
business owners with whom we've worked.

It is a belief that says small businesses in the United
States simply do not work; the people who own them
do.

And what we have also discovered is that the people
who own small businesses in this country work far
more than they should for the return they're getting.

Indeed, the problem is not that the owners of small
businesses in this country don't work; the problem is
that they're doing the wrong work.

As a result, most of their businesses end up in

chaos—unmanageable, unpredictable, and unrewarding.

Just look at the numbers.

Businesses start and fail in the United States at an increasingly staggering rate. Every year, over a million people in this country start a business of some sort. Statistics tell us that by the end of the first year at least 40 percent of them will be out of business.[1]

Within five years, more than 80 percent of them—800,000—will have failed.

And the rest of the bad news is, if you own a small business that has managed to survive for five years or more, don't breathe a sigh of relief. Because more than 80 percent of the small businesses that survive the first five years fail in the second five.

Why is this?

Why do so many people go into business, only to fail?

What lesson aren't they learning?

Why is it that with all the information available today on how to be successful in small business, so few people really are?

This book answers those questions.

It's about four profound ideas, which, if you understand and take them to heart, will give you the power to create an extraordinarily exciting, and personally rewarding, small business.

Ignore them, and you will likely join the hundreds of thousands of people every year who pour their energy and capital—and life—into starting a small business and fail, or the many others who struggle along for years simply trying to survive.

[1]Department of Commerce.

IDEA #1 There is a myth in this country—I call it the E-Myth—which says that small businesses are started by entrepreneurs risking capital to make a profit. This is simply not so. The real reasons people start businesses have little to do with entrepreneurship. In fact, this belief in the Entrepreneurial Myth is the most important factor in the devastating rate of small business failure today. Understanding the E-Myth, and applying that understanding to the creation and development of a small business, can be the secret to any business's success.

IDEA #2 There's a revolution going on today in American small business. I call it the Turn-Key Revolution. Not only is it changing the way we do business in this country and throughout the world but it is changing who goes into business, how they do it, and the likelihood of their survival.

IDEA #3 At the heart of the Turn-Key Revolution is a dynamic process we at E-Myth Worldwide call the Business Development Process. When it is systematized and applied purposely by a small business owner, the Business Development Process has the power to transform any small business into an incredibly effective organization. Our experience has shown us that when a small business incorporates this process into its every activity and uses it to control its destiny, that company stays young and thrives. When a small business ignores this process—as most unfortunately do—it commits itself to Management by Luck, stagnation, and, ultimately, failure. The consequences are inevitable.

IDEA #4   The Business Development Process can be systematically applied by any small business owner in a step-by-step method that incorporates the lessons of the Turn-Key Revolution into the operation of that business. This process then becomes a predictable way to produce results and vitality in any small business whose owner is willing to give it the time and attention it requires to flourish.

Since the founding of E-Myth Worldwide in 1977, we have assisted over 25,000 small business owners with the implementation of our Business Development Process through their enrollment in our unique E-Myth Mastery Program™, and I have seen it succeed thousands of times.

I would venture to guess that no organization has had more direct experience applying the lessons of the Turn-Key Revolution and the Business Development Process to the development of a small business than we have had at E-Myth Worldwide. And, while the process is no "magic bullet" and does require hard work, it is always gratifying work and the only work I know that will give you the level of control you need to get what you want from your small business. Indeed, it will change your business and it will change your life.

This book, then, is about producing results—not simply "how to do it." Because both of us know that books like that don't work. People do.

And what makes people work is an idea worth working for, along with a clear understanding of what needs to be done.

It is only when such an idea becomes firmly integrated into the way you think and operate your business that "how to do it" becomes meaningful.

This book is about such an idea—an idea that says your business is nothing more than a distinct reflection of who you are.

If your thinking is sloppy, your business will be sloppy.

If you are disorganized, your business will be disorganized.

If you are greedy, your employees will be greedy, giving you less and less of themselves and always asking for more.

If your information about what needs to be done in your business is limited, your business will reflect that limitation.

So if your business is to change—as it must continuously to thrive—you must change first. If you are unwilling to change, your business will never be capable of giving you what you want.

The first change that needs to take place has to do with your idea of what a business really is and what it takes to make one work.

Once you fully understand the relationship every owner must have with his or her business if it is to work, I can assure you that your business and your life will take on new vitality and new meaning.

You'll know why so many people fail to get what they want from a business of their own.

You'll see the almost magical opportunities available to anyone who starts a small business in the right way, with a true understanding, with the necessary tools.

I've seen it happen thousands of times, in every kind of business imaginable, with people who knew nothing about business when they started.

My wish is that by the time you are through reading this book, it will have started to happen to you.

PART I

The E-Myth and American Small Business

THE ENTREPRENEURIAL MYTH

They intoxicate themselves with work so they won't see how they really are.

Aldous Huxley

The E-Myth is the myth of the entrepreneur. It runs deep in this country and rings of the heroic.

Picture the typical entrepreneur and Herculean pictures come to mind: a man or woman standing alone, wind-blown against the elements, bravely defying insurmountable odds, climbing sheer faces of treacherous rock—all to realize the dream of creating a business of one's own.

The legend reeks of nobility, of lofty, extra-human efforts, of a prodigious commitment to larger-than-life ideals.

Well, while there are such people, my experience tells me they are rare.

Of the thousands of businesspeople I have had the opportunity to know and work with over the past two decades, few were *real* entrepreneurs when I met them.

The vision was all but gone in most.

The zest for the climb had turned into a terror of heights.

The face of the rock had become something to cling to rather than to scale.

Exhaustion was common, exhilaration rare.

But hadn't all of them once been entrepreneurs? After all, they had started their own business. There must have been some dream that drove them to take such a risk.

But, if so, where was the dream now? Why had it faded?

Where was the entrepreneur who had started the business?

The answer is simple: *the entrepreneur had only existed for a moment.*

A fleeting second in time.

And then it was gone. In most cases, forever.

If the entrepreneur survived at all, it was only as a myth that grew out of a misunderstanding about who goes into business and why.

A misunderstanding that has cost us dearly in this country—more than we can possibly imagine—in lost resources, lost opportunities, and wasted lives.

That myth, that misunderstanding, I call the E-Myth, the myth of the entrepreneur.

And it finds its roots in this country in a romantic belief that small businesses are started by entrepreneurs, when, in fact, most are not.

Then who does start small businesses in America?

And why?

The Entrepreneurial Seizure

To understand the E-Myth and the misunderstanding at its core, let's take a closer look at the person who goes into business. Not after he goes into business, but before.

For that matter, where were you before you started your business? And, if you're thinking about going into business, where are you now?

Well, if you're like most of the people I've known, you were working for somebody else.

What were you doing?

Probably technical work, like almost everybody who goes into business.

You were a carpenter, a mechanic, or a machinist.

You were a bookkeeper or a poodle clipper; a draftsperson or a hairdresser; a barber or a computer programmer; a doctor or a technical writer; a graphic artist or an accountant; an interior designer or a plumber or a salesperson.

But whatever you were, you were doing technical work.

And you were probably damn good at it.

But you were doing it for somebody else.

Then, one day, for no apparent reason, something happened. It might have been the weather, a birthday, or your child's graduation from high school. It might have been the paycheck you received on a Friday afternoon, or a sideways glance from the boss that just didn't sit right. It might have been a feeling that your boss didn't really appreciate your contribution to the success of his business.

It could have been anything; it doesn't matter what. But one day, for apparently no reason, *you were suddenly stricken with an Entrepreneurial Seizure.* And from that day on your life was never to be the same.

Inside your mind it sounded something like this: "What am I doing this for? Why am I working for this guy? Hell, I know as much about this business as he does. If it weren't for me, he wouldn't have a business. Any dummy can run a business. I'm working for one."

And the moment you paid attention to what you were saying and really took it to heart, your fate was sealed.

The excitement of cutting the cord became your constant companion.

The thought of independence followed you everywhere.

The idea of being your own boss, doing your own thing, singing your own song, became obsessively irresistible.

Once you were stricken with an Entrepreneurial Seizure, there was no relief.

You couldn't get rid of it.

You *had* to start your own business.

The Fatal Assumption

In the throes of your Entrepreneurial Seizure, you fell victim to the most disastrous assumption anyone can make about going into business.

It is an assumption made by all technicians who go into business for themselves, one that charts the course of a business—from Grand Opening to Liquidation—the moment it is made.

That Fatal Assumption is: *if you understand the technical work of a business, you understand a business that does that technical work.*

And the reason it's fatal is that it just isn't true.

In fact, it's the root cause of most small business failures!

The technical work of a business and a business that does that technical work *are two totally different things!*

But the technician who starts a business fails to see this.

To the technician suffering from an Entrepreneurial Seizure, a business is not a business but a place to go to work.

So the carpenter, or the electrician, or the plumber becomes a contractor.

The barber opens up a barber shop.

The technical writer starts a technical writing business.

The hairdresser starts a beauty salon.

The engineer goes into the semiconductor business.

The musician opens up a music store.

All of them believing that by understanding the technical work of the business they are immediately and eminently qualified to run a business that does that kind of work.

And it's simply not true!

In fact, rather than being their greatest single asset, knowing the technical work of their business becomes their greatest single liability.

For if the technician didn't know how to do the technical work of the business, he would have to learn how to get it done.

He would be forced to learn how to make the business work, rather than to do the work himself.

The real tragedy is that when the technician falls prey to the Fatal Assumption, the business that was supposed to free him from the limitations of working for somebody else actually enslaves him.

Suddenly the job he knew how to do so well becomes one job he knows how to do plus a dozen others he doesn't know how to do at all.

Because although the Entrepreneurial Seizure started the business, it's the technician who goes to work.

And suddenly, an entrepreneurial dream turns into a technician's nightmare.

See the Young Woman Baking Pies.
See the Young Woman Start a Business Baking Pies.
See the Young Woman Become an Old Woman.

I met Sarah after she had been in business for three years. She told me, "They have been the longest three years of my life."

Sarah's business was named All About Pies (not its real name).

But, in truth, Sarah's business wasn't really all about pies—it was really all about work. The work Sarah did. The work Sarah used to love to do more than anything else. Plus the work Sarah had never done in her life.

"In fact," Sarah said to me, "not only do I hate to do all this [she spread her arms, taking in the small shop in which we stood] but I *hate* [she emphasized the word almost fiercely]—I *hate* baking pies. I can't stand the thought of pies. I can't stand the smell of pies. I can't stand the sight of pies." And then she started crying.

The sweet fresh aroma of pies filled the air.

It was 7 A.M. and All About Pies was to open in thirty minutes. But Sarah's mind was someplace else.

"It's seven o'clock," she said, wiping her eyes with her apron, as though reading my mind. "Do you realize I've been here since three o'clock this morning? And that I was up at two to get ready? And that by the time I get the pies ready, open for business, take care of my customers, clean up, close up, do the shopping, reconcile the cash register, go to the bank, have dinner, and get the pies ready for tomorrow's bake, it'll be nine-thirty or ten o'clock tonight, and by the time I do all that, by the time any normal person, for God's sake, would say that the day was done, I will then also need to sit down and begin to figure out how I'm going to pay the rent next month?

"And all this [she spread her arms wearily again, as though to accentuate everything she had just said] because my very best friends told me I was crazy not to open a pie shop because I was so damn good at it? And, what's worse, I believed them! I saw a way out of the horrible job I used to have. I saw a way to get free, doing work I loved to do, and doing it all for me."

She was on a tear that I didn't want to interrupt. I waited quietly to hear what she would say next.

Instead, she kicked the huge black oven in front of her with her right foot.

"Damn!" she exploded.

"Damn, Damn, Damn!"

For emphasis, she kicked the oven again. And then slumped, sighed deeply, and hugged herself, almost desperately.

"What do I do now?" she said, almost in a whisper.

Not really asking me, I knew, but asking herself.

Sarah leaned against the wall and remained there quietly for a long moment, staring at her feet. The large clock on the wall ticked loudly in the empty shop. I could hear the cars driving by on the busy street in front of the shop as the city came awake. The sun shone harshly through the spotless windows, sweeping the gleaming oak floor in front of the counter.

I could see the dust in the stream of light, hanging suspended as though waiting for Sarah to speak.

She was deep in debt.

She had spent everything she had, and more, to create this lovely little shop.

The floors were the best oak.

The ovens were the best ovens.

The displays were charming, the very best money could buy.

She had put her heart into this place, just as she had put her heart into her pies, falling in love with baking as a young girl, mentored by her aunt who had lived with her family while Sarah was growing up.

Her aunt had filled her family's kitchen, Sarah's childhood, with the delicious, sweet aroma of freshly baked pies. Her aunt had introduced her to the magic of the process: the kneading of the dough, the cleaning of the oven, the sprinkling of the flour, the preparation of the trays, the careful cutting of the apples, the cherries, the rhubarb, the peaches. It was a labor of love.

Her aunt had corrected her when, in her haste, Sarah had hurried the process.

Her aunt had told her, time and time again, "Sarah, dear, we have all the time in the world. Baking pies is not about getting done. It's about baking pies."

And Sarah thought she understood her.

But now Sarah knew that baking pies was about "getting done." Baking pies was ruined for her. At least she thought it was.

The clock continued its emphatic ticking.

I watched as Sarah seemed to shrink even closer to herself.

I knew how oppressive it must be for her to find herself so deeply in debt, to feel so helpless in the face of it. Where was her aunt now? Who was going to teach her what to do next?

"Sarah," I said as carefully as I could.

"It's time to learn all about pies all over again."

The technician suffering from an Entrepreneurial Seizure takes the work he loves to do and turns it into a job. The work that was born out of love becomes a chore, among a welter of other less familiar and less pleasant chores. Rather than maintaining its specialness, representing the unique skill the technician possesses and upon which he started the business, the work becomes trivialized, something to get through in order to make room for everything else that must be done.

I told Sarah that every technician suffering from an Entrepreneurial Seizure experiences exactly the same thing.

First, exhilaration; second, terror; third, exhaustion; and, finally, despair. A terrible sense of loss—not only the loss of what was closest to them, their special relationship with their work, but the loss of purpose, the loss of self.

Sarah looked at me with a sense of relief, as though she felt seen but not judged.

"You've got my number," she said. "But what do I do now?"

"You take this one step at a time," I answered.

"The technician isn't the only problem you've got to deal with here."

2

THE ENTREPRENEUR, THE MANAGER, AND THE TECHNICIAN

Thus, in the course of his life, one man acquires many personal qualities, many personages, many 'I's' (because each, speaking for itself independently of the others says 'I,' 'me,' when it appears).

Jean Vaysse
Toward Awakening

No, The Technician isn't the only problem. The problem is more complicated than that.

The problem is that everybody who goes into business is actually three-people-in-one: The Entrepreneur, The Manager, and The Technician.

And the problem is compounded by the fact that while each of these personalities wants to be the boss, none of them wants to have a boss.

So they start a business together in order to get rid of the boss. And the conflict begins.

To show you how the problem manifests itself in all of us, let's examine the way our various internal personalities interact. Let's take a look at two personalities we're all familiar with: The Fat Guy and The Skinny Guy.

Have you ever decided to go on a diet?

You're sitting in front of the television set one Saturday afternoon, watching an athletic competition, awed by the athletes' stamina and dexterity.

You're eating a sandwich, your second since you sat down to watch the event two hours before.

You're feeling sluggish in the face of all the action on the screen when, suddenly, somebody wakes up in you and says, "What are you doing? Look at yourself, You're Fat! You're out of shape! Do something about it!"

It has happened to us all. Somebody wakes up inside us with a totally different picture of who we should be and what we should be doing. In this case, let's call him The Skinny Guy.

Who's The Skinny Guy? He's the one who uses words like *discipline, exercise, organization.* The Skinny Guy is intolerant, self-righteous, a stickler for detail, a compulsive tyrant.

The Skinny Guy abhors fat people. Can't stand sitting around. Needs to be on the move. Lives for action.

The Skinny Guy has just taken over. Watch out—things are about to change.

Before you know it, you're cleaning all the fattening foods out of the refrigerator. You're buying a new pair of running shoes, barbells, and sweats. Things are going to be different around here. You have a new lease on life. You plan your new physical regimen: up at five, run three miles, cold shower at six, a breakfast of wheat toast, black coffee, and half a grapefruit; then, ride your bicycle to work, home by seven, run another two miles, to bed at ten—the world's already a different place!

And you actually pull it off! By Monday night, you've lost two pounds. You go to sleep dreaming of winning the Boston Marathon. Why not? The way things are going, it's only a matter of time.

Tuesday night you get on the scale. Another pound gone! You're incredible. Gorgeous. A lean machine.

On Wednesday, you really pour it on. You work out an extra hour in the morning, an extra half-hour at night.

You can't wait to get on the scale. You strip down to your bare skin, shivering in the bathroom, filled with expectation of what your scale is going to tell you. You step lightly onto it and look down. What you see is . . . *nothing*. You haven't lost an ounce. You're exactly the same as you were on Tuesday.

Dejection creeps in. You begin to feel a slight twinge of resentment. "After all that work? After all that sweat and effort? And then—nothing? It isn't fair." But you shrug it off. After all, tomorrow's another day. You go to bed, vowing to work harder on Thursday. But somehow something has changed.

You don't know what's changed until Thursday morning.

It's raining.

The room is cold.

Something feels different.

What is it?

For a minute or two you can't quite put your finger on it.

And then you get it: *somebody else is in your body.*

It's The Fat Guy!

He's back!

And he doesn't want to run.

As a matter of fact, he doesn't even want to get out of bed. It's cold outside. "Run? Are you kidding me?" The Fat Guy doesn't want anything to do with it. The only exercise he might be interested in is eating!

And all of a sudden you find yourself in front of the refrigerator—*inside* the refrigerator—all over the kitchen!

Food is now your major interest.

The Marathon is gone; the lean machine is gone; the sweats and barbells and running shoes are gone.

The Fat Guy is back. He's running the show again.

It happens to all of us, time and time again. Because we've been deluded into thinking we're really *one person.*

And so when The Skinny Guy decides to change things we actually believe that it's *I* who's making that decision.

And when The Fat Guy wakes up and changes it all back again, we think it's *I* who's making that decision too.

But it isn't I. It's *we.*

The Skinny Guy and The Fat Guy are two totally different personalities, with different needs, different interests, and different lifestyles.

That's why they don't like each other. They each want totally different things.

The problem is that when you're The Skinny Guy, you're totally consumed by *his* needs, *his* interests, *his* lifestyle.

And then something happens—the scale disappoints you, the weather turns cold, somebody offers you a ham sandwich.

At that moment, The Fat Guy, who's been waiting in the wings all this time, grabs your attention. Grabs control.

You're him again.

In other words, when you're The Skinny Guy you're always making promises for The Fat Guy to keep.

And when you're The Fat Guy, you're always making promises for The Skinny Guy to keep.

Is it any wonder we have such a tough time keeping our commitments to ourselves?

It's not that we're indecisive or unreliable; it's that each and every one of us is a whole set of different personalities, each with his own interests and way of doing things. Asking any one of them to defer to any of the others is inviting a battle or even a full-scale war.

Anyone who has ever experienced the conflict between The Fat Guy and The Skinny Guy (and haven't we all?) knows what I mean. You can't be both; one of them has to lose. And they both know it.

Well, that's the kind of war going on inside the owner of every small business.

But it's a three-way battle between The Entrepreneur, The Manager, and The Technician.

Unfortunately, it's a battle no one can win.

Understanding the differences between them will quickly explain why.

The Entrepreneur

The entrepreneurial personality turns the most trivial condition into an exceptional opportunity. The Entrepreneur is the visionary in us. The dreamer. The energy behind every human activity. The imagination that sparks the fire of the future. The catalyst for change.

The Entrepreneur lives in the future, never in the past, rarely in the present. He's happiest when left free to construct images of "what-if" and "if-when."

In science, the entrepreneurial personality works in the most abstract and least pragmatic areas of particle physics, pure mathematics, and theoretical astronomy. In art, it thrives in the rarefied arena of the avant-garde. In business, The Entrepreneur is the innovator, the grand strategist, the creator of new methods for penetrating or creating new markets, the world-bending giant—like Sears Roebuck, Henry Ford, Tom Watson of IBM, and Ray Kroc of McDonald's.

The Entrepreneur is our creative personality—always at its best dealing with the unknown, prodding the future, creating probabilities out of possibilities, engineering chaos into harmony.

Every strong entrepreneurial personality has an extraordinary need for control. Living as he does in the visionary world of the future, he needs control of people and events in the present so that he can concentrate on his dreams.

Given his need for change, The Entrepreneur creates a great deal of havoc around him, which is predictably unsettling for those he enlists in his projects.

As a result, he often finds himself rapidly outdistancing the others.

The farther ahead he is, the greater the effort required to pull his cohorts along.

This then becomes the entrepreneurial worldview: a world made up of both an overabundance of opportunities and dragging feet.

The problem is, how can he pursue the opportunities without getting mired down by the feet?

The way he usually chooses is to bully, harass, excoriate, flatter, cajole, scream, and finally, when all else fails, promise whatever he must to keep the project moving.

To The Entrepreneur, most people are problems that get in the way of the dream.

The Manager

The managerial personality is pragmatic. Without The Manager there would be no planning, no order, no predictability.

The Manager is the part of us that goes to Sears and buys stacking plastic boxes, takes them back to the garage, and systematically stores all the various sized nuts, bolts, and screws in their own carefully identified drawer. He then hangs all of the tools in impeccable order on the walls—lawn tools on one wall, carpentry tools on another—and, to be absolutely certain that order is not disturbed, paints a picture of each tool on the wall where it hangs!

If The Entrepreneur lives in the future, The Manager lives in the past.

Where The Entrepreneur craves control, The Manager craves order.

Where The Entrepreneur thrives on change, The Manager compulsively clings to the status quo.

Where The Entrepreneur invariably sees the opportunity in events, The Manager invariably sees the problems.

The Manager builds a house and then lives in it, forever.

The Entrepreneur builds a house and the instant it's done begins planning the next one.

The Manager creates neat, orderly rows of things. The Entrepreneur creates the things The Manager puts in rows.

The Manager is the one who runs after The Entrepreneur to clean up the mess. Without The Entrepreneur there would be no mess to clean up.

Without The Manager, there could be no business, no society. Without The Entrepreneur, there would be no innovation.

It is the tension between The Entrepreneur's vision and The Manager's pragmatism that creates the synthesis from which all great works are born.

The Technician

The Technician is the doer.

"If you want it done right, do it yourself" is The Technician's credo.

The Technician loves to tinker. Things are to be taken apart and put back together again. Things aren't supposed to be dreamed about, they're supposed to be done.

If The Entrepreneur lives in the future and The Manager lives in the past, The Technician lives in the present. He loves the feel of things and the fact that things can get done.

As long as The Technician is working, he is happy, but only on one thing at a time. He knows that two things can't get done simultaneously; only a fool would try. So he works steadily and is happiest when he is in control of the work flow.

As a result, The Technician mistrusts those he works for, because they are always trying to get more work done than is either possible or necessary.

To The Technician, thinking is unproductive unless it's thinking about the work that needs to be done.

As a result, he is suspicious of lofty ideas or abstractions.

Thinking isn't work; it gets in the way of work.

The Technician isn't interested in ideas; he's interested in "how to do it."

To The Technician, all ideas need to be reduced to methodology if they are to be of any value. And with good reason.

The Technician knows that if it weren't for him, the world would be in more trouble than it already is. Nothing would get done, but lots of people would be *thinking* about it.

Put another way, while The Entrepreneur dreams, The Manager frets, and The Technician ruminates.

The Technician is a resolute individualist, standing his ground, producing today's bread to eat at tonight's dinner. He is the backbone of every cultural tradition, but most importantly, of ours. If The Technician didn't do it, it wouldn't get done.

Everyone gets in The Technician's way.

The Entrepreneur is always throwing a monkey wrench into his day with the creation of yet another "great new idea."

On the other hand, The Entrepreneur is always creating new and interesting work for The Technician to do, thus establishing a potentially symbiotic relationship.

Unfortunately, it rarely works out that way.

Since most entrepreneurial ideas don't work in the

real world, The Technician's usual experience is one of frustration and annoyance at being interrupted in the course of doing what *needs* to be done to try something new that probably doesn't need to be done at all.

The Manager is also a problem to The Technician because he is determined to impose order on The Technician's work, to reduce him to a part of "the system."

But being a rugged individualist, The Technician can't stand being treated that way.

To The Technician, "the system" is dehumanizing, cold, antiseptic, and impersonal. It violates his individuality.

Work is what a *person* does. And to the degree that it's not, work becomes something foreign.

To The Manager, however, work is a system of results in which The Technician is but a component part.

To The Manager, then, The Technician becomes a problem to be managed. To The Technician, The Manager becomes a meddler to be avoided.

To both of them, The Entrepreneur is the one who got them into trouble in the first place!

The fact of the matter is that we all have an Entrepreneur, Manager, and Technician inside us. And if they were equally balanced, we'd be describing an incredibly competent individual.

The Entrepreneur would be free to forge ahead into new areas of interest; The Manager would be solidifying the base of operations; and The Technician would be doing the technical work.

Each would derive satisfaction from the work he

does best, serving the whole in the most productive way.

Unfortunately, our experience shows us that few people who go into business are blessed with such a balance. Instead, the typical small business owner is only 10 percent Entrepreneur, 20 percent Manager, and 70 percent Technician.

The Entrepreneur wakes up with a vision.

The Manager screams "Oh, no!"

And while the two of them are battling it out, The Technician seizes the opportunity to go into business for himself.

Not to pursue the entrepreneurial dream, however, but to finally wrest control of his work from the other two.

To The Technician it's a dream come true. The Boss is dead.

But to the business it's a disaster, because the wrong person is at the helm.

The Technician is in charge!

Sarah looked a little overwhelmed.

"I don't understand," she said. "How could I have done this differently? The only reason I went into this business was because I loved baking pies. If it hadn't been for that, what would have been the point?" She watched my face suspiciously, as though I were trying to make her already impossible situation even more impossible.

"Well, let's think about it together," I answered.

"If it's true that within each businessperson there are three personalities, rather than just one, can you imagine what a mess that makes? If one of you wants this, and another of you wants that, and a third wants something entirely different, can you imagine the confusion that causes in our lives? And it's not only the personalities inside each one of us that confuse us but all the others we come into contact with as well: in our customers, in our employees, in our children, in our partners, in our parents, in our friends, in our spouses, in our lovers. If this is true, and all you need to do to discover whether it is or not is to take a look at yourself from day to day, as though from above, as though from outside of your skin, as though you were watching someone else—that is, to observe yourself as you go through the day—you would see the different parts come out. You would see them playing their respective games. You would see how they fight for their own space—and the space of all the others—and sabotage each other as best they can.

"In your business, you would see how one part of you craves a sense of order, while another part of you dreams about the future. You would see how another part of you can't stand being idle, and jumps in to bake, and to clean up, and to wait on customers, the part of you who feels guilty if she isn't doing something all the time.

"In short, you would see how The Entrepreneur in you dreams and schemes, The Manager in you is constantly attempting to keep things as they are, and The Technician in you drives the other two crazy. You would see that it not only matters that your personalities are not in a balanced relationship with each other but that your life depends on gaining that balance. That until you do, it's a war! And it's a war no one can win.

"You would also see that one of your personalities is

the strongest of the three (or four, or five, or six), and that she always manages to control the others. In fact, if you watch long enough, you'll begin to understand how devastating the tyranny of your strongest personality is to your life. And you'll see that without balance, without all three of these personalities being given the opportunity, the freedom, the nourishment they each need to grow, your business cannot help but mirror your own lopsidedness.

"So it is that an entrepreneurial business, without a Manager to give it order and without a Technician to put it to work, is doomed to suffer an early, and probably very dramatic, death. And that a Manager-driven business, without an Entrepreneur or a Technician to play their absolutely critical roles, will put things into little gray boxes over and over again, only to realize too late that there's no reason for the things or the boxes she put them into! Such a business will die very neatly.

"And that in a Technician-driven business, without The Entrepreneur to lead her and The Manager to supervise her, The Technician will work until she drops, only to wake up the next morning to go to work even harder, and the next, and the next. Only to discover, long after it's too late, that while she was working someone moved a freeway through the store!"

Sarah looked at me with uncertainty.

"But, I'm not an Entrepreneur," she said.

"All I do is bake pies. All I ever wanted to do was to bake pies, just like The Technician you described. When entrepreneurial personalities were passed out, I think I got passed over. What do I do if there is no Entrepreneur in me?"

I couldn't help but smile. This was going to be fun.

Because I knew when Sarah finally got it—and I knew she would—she was going to discover someone in herself she never knew was there.

"Before we reach that conclusion, Sarah, let's look more closely at what an Entrepreneur does," I responded.

"An Entrepreneur does the work of envisioning the business as something apart from you, the owner. The work of asking all the right questions about *why* this business, as opposed to that business? Why a pie baking business rather than a body shop? If you are a baker of pies, it's easy for you to decide to open up a pie-baking business. But that's just the point. If you are a baker of pies and are determined to do entrepreneurial work, you would leave your pie-baking experience behind you and engage in the internal dialogue with which every truly entrepreneurial personality is wonderfully familiar.

"You would begin to say to yourself, 'It's time for me to create a new life. It's time for me to challenge my imagination and to begin the process of shaping an entirely new life. And the best way to do that anywhere in this whole wide opportunity-filled world is to create an exciting new business. One that can give me everything that I want, one that doesn't require me to be there all the time, one that has the potential to be stunningly unique, one that people will talk about long after having shopped in it the very first time, and, as a result of that delightful experience, will come back to shop there again because it has such a special flavor to it. I wonder what that business would be?'

"I wonder what that business would be?" I said to Sarah, "is the truly entrepreneurial question. The dreaming question, I call it. It's the question that is at the heart of the work of an Entrepreneur. I wonder. I wonder. I wonder.

"So the work of an Entrepreneur is to wonder," I continued. "To imagine and to dream. To see with as much of herself as she can muster the possibilities that waft about in midair someplace there above her head and within her heart. Not in the past but in the future. That's the work the entrepreneurial personality does at the outset of her business and at each and every stage along the way. I wonder. I wonder. I wonder. Just as every inventor must. Just as every composer must. Just as every artist, or every craftsperson, or every physicist must. Just as every baker of pies must. I call it Future Work. 'I wonder' is the true work of the entrepreneurial personality."

She tried to repress it, but I saw a small smile begin to form on Sarah's mouth.

"How could I do this differently," she finally asked me with growing confidence. "If I were to give the true entrepreneur in myself life, how could I totally change my experience of this business?"

"Now you've got it!" I said. "That's just the right question. And to get to the answer, let's look at where your business exists today in the small business life cycle."

3

INFANCY:
THE TECHNICIAN'S PHASE

. . . my Uncle Sol had a skunk farm but the skunks
caught cold and died and so my Uncle Sol imitated the
skunks in a subtle manner . . .

e. e. cummings
Collected Poems

It is self-evident that businesses, like people, are supposed to grow; and with growth, comes change.

Unfortunately, most businesses are not run according to this principle. Instead most businesses are operated according to what the *owner* wants as opposed to
what the *business* needs.

And what The Technician who runs the company
wants is not growth or change but exactly the opposite.
He wants a place to go to work, free to do what he
wants, when he wants, free from the constraints of
working for The Boss.

Unfortunately, what The Technician wants dooms
his business before it even begins.

To understand why, let's take a look at the three

phases of a business's growth: Infancy, Adolescence, and Maturity.

Understanding each phase, and what goes on in the business owner's mind during each of them, is critical to discovering why most small businesses don't thrive and ensuring that yours does.

The Boss is dead, and you, The Technician, are free at last. Finally, you can do your own thing in your own business. Hope runs high. The air is electric with possibility. It's like being let out of school for the summer. Your newfound freedom is intoxicating.

In the beginning nothing is too much for your business to ask. As The Technician, you're accustomed to "paying your dues." So the hours devoted to the business during Infancy are not spent grudgingly but optimistically. There's work to be done, and that's what you're all about. After all, your middle name is Work. "Besides," you think, "this work is for me."

And so you work. Ten, twelve, fourteen hours a day. Seven days a week. Even when you're at home, you're at work. All your thoughts, all your feelings, revolve around your new business. You can't get it out of your mind. You're consumed by it; totally invested in doing whatever is necessary to keep it alive.

But now you're doing not only the work you know how to do but the work you don't know how to do as well. You're not only making it but you're also buying it, selling it, and shipping it. During Infancy, you're a Master Juggler, keeping all the balls in the air.

It's easy to spot a business in Infancy—*the owner and the business are one and the same thing*.

If you removed the owner from an Infancy business,

there would be no business left. It would disappear!

In Infancy, you *are* the business.

It's even named after you—"JOE'S PLACE," "TOMMY'S JOINT," "MARY'S FINE FOODS"—so the customer won't forget you're The Boss.

And soon—if you're lucky—all of the sweat, worry, and work begin to pay off. You're good. You work hard. The customers don't forget. They're coming back. They're sending in friends. Their friends have friends. And they're all talking about Joe, Tommy, and Mary. They're all talking about you.

If you can believe what your customers are saying, there's never been anyone like Joe, Tommy, and Mary. Joe, Tommy, and Mary are just like old friends. They work hard for their money. And they do good work. Joe is the best barber I ever went to. Tommy is the best printer I ever used. Mary makes the best corned beef sandwich I ever ate. Your customers are crazy about you. They keep coming, in droves.

And you love it!

But then it changes. Subtly at first, but gradually it becomes obvious. You're falling behind. There's more work to do than you can possibly get done. The customers are relentless. They want you; they need you. You've spoiled them for anyone else. You're working at breakneck speed.

And then the inevitable happens. You, the Master Juggler, begin to drop some of the balls!

It can't be helped. No matter how hard you try, you simply can't catch them all. Your enthusiasm for working with the customers wanes. Deliveries, once early, are now late. The product begins to show the wear and tear. Nothing seems to work the way it did at first.

Joe's haircuts don't look the way they used to. "I said short in the back, not on the sides." "My name's not Fred; that's my brother—and I never had a crewcut!"

Glitches start showing up in Tommy's printing: typos, ink smudges, wrong colors, wrong paper. "I didn't order business cards; I ordered catalog covers." "Pink? I said brown!"

Mary's best-tasting-biggest-stack-of-corned-beef-in-the-world suddenly looks like pastrami. It is pastrami. "Didn't you ask for pastrami?" Another irritated voice calls out: "Where's my pastrami sandwich? This is corned beef!" And yet another: "What are these garbanzo beans doing in my meatloaf?"

What do you do? You stretch. You work harder. You put in more time, more energy.

If you put in twelve hours before, you now put in fourteen.

If you put in fourteen hours before, you now put in sixteen.

If you put in sixteen hours before, you now put in twenty. But the balls keep dropping!

All of a sudden, Joe, Tommy, and Mary wish their names weren't on the sign.

All of a sudden, they want to hide.

All of a sudden, you find yourself at the end of an unbelievably hectic week, late on a Saturday night, poring over the books, trying to make some sense out of the mess, thinking about all of the work you didn't get done this week, and all of the work waiting for you next week. And you suddenly realize *it simply isn't going to get done.* There's simply no way in the world you can do all that work yourself!

In a flash, you realize that your business has become

The Boss you thought you left behind. *There's no getting rid of the Boss!*

Infancy ends when the owner realizes that the business cannot continue to run the way it has been; that, in order for it to survive, it will have to change.

When that happens—when the reality sinks in—most business failures occur.

When that happens, most of The Technicians lock their doors behind them and walk away.

The rest go on to Adolescence.

Sarah was beginning to look defeated again. I had seen that look before on the faces of countless clients. When a Technician-turned-business-owner is suddenly confronted with the reality of her situation, a sense of hopelessness can set in. The challenge can seem overwhelming. But, I sensed that Sarah would struggle with the idea—and herself—until she got it.

"I guess I still don't get it," she said. "What's wrong with being a Technician? I used to love the work I do. And if I didn't have to do all these other things, I would still love it!"

"Of course you would," I answered. "And that's exactly the point!

"There's nothing wrong with being a Technician. There's only something wrong with being a Technician who also owns a business! Because as a Technician-turned-business-owner, your focus is upside down. You see the world from the bottom up rather than from the top down. You have a tactical view rather than a strategic view. You see the work that has to get done, and because of the way you're built, you immediately jump in to do it! You believe that a business is nothing more than an aggregate of the various types of work done in it, when in fact it is much more than that.

"If you want to work in a business, get a job in somebody else's business! But don't go to work in your own. Because while you're working, while you're answering the telephone, while you're baking pies, while you're cleaning the windows and the floors, while you're doing it, doing it, doing it, there's something much more important that isn't getting done. And it's the work you're not doing, the strategic work, the entrepreneurial work, that will lead your business forward, that will give you the life you've not yet known.

"No," I said, truly enjoying this, "there's nothing wrong with technical work; it is, it can be, pure joy.

"It's only a problem when The Technician consumes all the other personalities. When The Technician fills your day with work. When The Technician avoids the challenge of learning how to grow a business. When The Technician shrinks from the entrepreneurial role so necessary to the lifeblood, the momentum, of a truly extraordinary small business, and from the managerial role so critical to the operational balance or grounding of a small business on a day-to-day basis.

"To be a great Technician is simply insufficient to the task of building a great small business. Being consumed by the tactical work of the business, as every Technician suffering from an Entrepreneurial Seizure is, leads to only one thing: a complicated, frustrating, and, eventually, demeaning job!

"I know you know what that feels like, Sarah. Can you see that as long as you view your business from The Technician's perspective, you are doomed to continue having this experience?" I asked her as gently as I could.

I saw that Sarah was still struggling with the idea of doing what she does differently. I waited for the question I knew was brewing, and it wasn't long before it came.

"But I can't even *imagine* what my business would be like without me doing the work," she said. "It has always depended on me. If it weren't for me, my customers would go someplace else. I'm not sure I understand what's really wrong with that."

"Well, think about it," I said. "In a business that depends on you, on your style, on your personality, on your presence, on your talent and willingness to do the work, if you're not there why of course your customers would go someplace else. Wouldn't you?

"Because in a business like that what your customers are buying is not your business's ability to give them what they want but *your* ability to give them what they want. And that's what's wrong with it!

"What if you don't want to be there? What if you'd like to be someplace else? On a vacation? Or at home? Reading a book? Working in the garden? Or on a sabbatical, for God's sake? Isn't there any place you would rather be at times than in your business, filling the needs of your customers who need you so badly because you're the only one who can do it?

"What if you're sick, or feel like being sick? Or what if you just feel lazy?

"Don't you see? If your business depends on you, you don't own a business—you have a job. And it's the worst job in the world because you're working for a lunatic!

"And, besides, that's not the purpose of going into business.

"The purpose of going into business is to get free of a job so you can create jobs for other people.

"The purpose of going into business is to expand beyond your existing horizons. So you can invent something that satisfies a need in the marketplace that has never been satisfied before. So you can live an expanded, stimulating new life."

Sarah said, "I hate to beat a dead horse, but what if I want to do the technical work in my business? What if I don't want to do anything else but that?"

"Then for God's sake," I said as emphatically as I dared, "get rid of your business! And get rid of it as quickly as you can. Because you can't have it both ways. You can't 'have your pie and eat it too.' You can't ignore the financial accountabilities, the marketing accountabilities, the sales and administrative accountabilities. You can't ignore your future employees' need for leadership, for purpose, for responsible management, for effective communication, for something more than just a job in which their sole purpose is to support you doing your job. Let alone what your business needs from you if it's to thrive: that you understand the way a business works, that you understand the dynamics of a business—cash flow, growth, customer sensitivity, competitive sensitivity, and so forth.

"The point is," I said to her, watching her face sink and then begin to lift with an unexpressed question, "if all you want from a business of your own is the opportunity to do what you did before you started your business, get paid more for it, and have more freedom to come and go, your greed—I know that sounds harsh, but that's what it is—your self-indulgence will eventually consume both you and your business."

I paused and then continued because I could see that Sarah was not yet totally convinced.

"You just can't get there from here! You just can't play the role of The Technician and ignore the roles of The Entrepreneur and The Manager simply because you're unprepared to play them.

"Because, the moment you chose to start a small business, Sarah, you unwittingly chose to play a significantly larger game than any game you had ever played before.

"And to play this new game, called *building a small business that actually works,* your Entrepreneur needs to be coaxed out, nourished, and given the room she needs to expand, and your Manager needs to be supported as well so she can develop her skill at creating order and translating the entrepreneurial vision into actions that can be efficiently manifested in the real world.

"Anything less than that will eventually push you to the brink of disaster and, finally, over the edge. Because a small business simply demands that we do it or the business will shrivel on the vine.

"So whether we like it or not, we have to learn how. The exciting thing is, that once you begin to, once your Technician begins to let go, once you make room for the rest of you to flourish, the game becomes more rewarding than you can possibly imagine at this point in your business's life."

"Tell me more about that," Sarah said. "I really want to know."

"I will," I answered. "Although I sense that you already understand quite a bit more than you think. But first, let's go on to Adolescence, the second stage in a small business's growth."

4

ADOLESCENCE:
GETTING SOME HELP

As governments, we stumble from crisis to crash program, lurching into the future without plan, without hope, without vision.

Alvin Toffler
The Third Wave

Adolescence begins at the point in the life of your business when you decide to get some help.

There's no telling how soon this will happen. But it *always* happens, precipitated by a crisis in the Infancy stage.

Every business that lasts must grow into the Adolescent phase. Every small business owner who survives seeks help.

What kind of help do you, the overloaded Technician, go out to get?

The answer is as easy as it is inevitable: *technical help.*

Someone with experience.

Someone with experience in your kind of business.

Someone who knows how to do the technical work that isn't getting done—usually the work you don't like to do.

The sales-oriented owner goes out to find a production person.

The production-oriented owner looks for a salesperson.

And just about everybody tries to find someone to do the books! Because if there's anything most small business owners hate to do—and therefore ignore—it's the books.

And so it is that you bring in your first employee—Harry, a sixty-eight-year-old bookkeeper who's been doing the books since he was twelve years old, in the Old Country.

Harry knows the books.

He knows how to do the books in eight different languages.

But most important, Harry has twenty-two years of experience doing the books in a company just like yours.

There is nothing Harry doesn't know about your kind of business.

And now he's yours.

The world suddenly looks brighter again.

A major ball is about to be caught—and by somebody else for a change!

It's Monday morning. Harry arrives. You greet him warmly, and, let's face it, feverishly. You've spent all weekend getting ready for this moment. You cleared out a generous space for him. You arranged the books and the stack of unopened letters on his desk. You bought a coffee cup with "Harry" printed on it. You were even thoughtful enough to find a cushion for his chair (he'll be sitting for a long time).

There's a critical moment in every business when the owner hires his very first employee to do the work he doesn't know how to do himself, or doesn't want to do. In your business, Harry is that person. And this Monday morning is that critical time.

Think about it.

You've taken a big step. The books are on Harry's desk now rather than yours.

And what's more, Harry is about to become the only other person in the whole world who knows the real story about you and your business.

Harry is going to take one look at the books and know the truth.

Harry, your very first and most important employee, is about to find out a secret you've been hiding from everyone else in your life: *that you don't know what you're doing!*

The question is, what's he going to do about it?

Will he laugh?

Will he cry?

Will he leave?

Or will he go to work?

And if Harry won't do the books, who will?

But suddenly you hear the quiet, systematic clattering of the calculator's keys from Harry's desk.

He's working!

Harry's going to stay!

You can't believe your luck.

You're not going to have to do the books anymore.

And in a single stroke, you suddenly understand what it means to be in business in a way you never understood before.

"I don't have to do that anymore!"

At last you're free. The Manager in you wakes up and The Technician temporarily goes to sleep. Your worries are over. Someone else is going to do that now.

But at the same time—unaccustomed as you are to being The Manager—your newfound freedom takes on an all too common form.

It's called *Management by Abdication* rather than by *Delegation.*

In short, like every small business owner has done before you, you hand the books over to Harry . . . and run.

And for a while you *are* free. At least relatively so. After all, you still have all the other work to do.

But now that you have Harry, things are beginning to change.

Because when Harry's not totally immersed in the books, you can get him to answer the phone.

And when he's not answering the phone, you can get him to do a little shipping and receiving.

And when he's not doing the shipping and receiving, he might as well handle a few of your customers.

And when he's not handling a few of your customers, well, who knows what you could think of next?

Life becomes easier. Life becomes a dream.

You begin to take a little longer lunch: thirty minutes instead of fifteen.

You leave a little earlier at the end of the day: eight o'clock instead of nine.

Harry comes to you occasionally to tell you what he needs, and you, busy as usual, simply tell him to handle it. How doesn't matter as long as he doesn't bother you with the details. You've got other fish to fry.

Harry needs more people. The business is beginning

to grow. Busy as usual, you tell him to hire them. He does. Harry's a wonder. It's great to have a guy like Harry. You don't have to think about what he's doing; you don't have to worry about how he's getting along. He never complains. He just works. And he's doing all the work you hate to do. It's the best of all possible worlds. You get to be The Boss, doing the work you love to do, and Harry takes care of everything else. Ah, the life of an Entrepreneur!

And then it unexpectedly happens.

A customer calls to complain about the shabby treatment she received from one of your people. "Who was it?" you ask, privately steaming. She doesn't know, but if you're going to hire people like that she'll take her business elsewhere.

You promise to look into it.

Your banker calls to tell you that you're overdrawn. "How did that happen?" you ask him, your heart dropping to your knees. He doesn't know, but if you don't watch it more closely he'll have to "take steps."

You promise to look into it.

Your oldest supplier calls to tell you that the order you placed the week before was placed wrong, so the shipment will be ten weeks late. What's more, you're going to have to eat the overage. "How did that happen?" you ask him, reaching for a Rolaid. He doesn't know, but if you can't manage your ordering better than that, he'll have to look at other options.

You promise to look into it.

Out on the shipping dock, you walk up to a kid Harry hired. He's wrapping a package. You look at the package and explode. "Who taught you to wrap a package like this?" you ask the surprised kid. "Didn't anyone show you how to do this right? Here, give it to me. I'll do it myself."

And you do.

That very afternoon, you happen to be walking by the production line. You almost drop in your tracks. "Who taught you to do it that way?" you stammer to the shocked production person. "Didn't anybody show you how to do it right? Here, give it to me. I'll do it myself."

And you do.

The very next morning, you're talking to the new salesperson, also hired by Harry.

"What's happening to customer A?" you ask her. Her answer sends you into a rage. "When I took care of him we never had problems like that!" you wail. "Here, give it to me. I'll take care of it myself."

And you do.

And the young shipping clerk looks at the production person, and they both look at the new salesperson, and they all look at their Acting Boss Harry, and ask: "Who the hell was that?!" Harry just shrugs and says (as only a man who's worked for other people for fifty-plus years can say): "Oh, that was just The Boss."

But, hear this: *what Harry knows is something you're about to learn.*

That it's only the beginning of a process that occurs in every Adolescent business once the owner's Management by Abdication begins to take its toll. It's only the beginning of a process of deterioration in which the number of balls in the air not only exceeds your ability to juggle them effectively but your people's ability as well.

What Harry knows, and what you're about to learn, is that it's only the beginning of a process in which the balls begin to fall faster and with greater frequency than they ever did when you were doing everything yourself.

And as the thud of the landing balls becomes deafening, you begin to realize that you never should have trusted Harry.

You never should have trusted anyone.

You should have known better.

As the balls continue to fall at an overwhelming rate, you begin to realize that no one cares about your business the way you do.

That no one is willing to work as hard as you work.

That no one has your judgment, or your ability, or your desire, or your interest.

That if it's going to get done right, you're the one who's going to have to do it.

So you run back into your business to become the Master Juggler again. It's the same old story. Walk into any Adolescent business anywhere in the world and you'll find the owner of the business doing it, doing it, doing it, busy, busy, busy—doing everything that has to get done in his business—despite the fact that he now has people who are supposed to be doing it for him. People he's paying to do it!

And what's worse is that the more he does, the less they do.

And the less they do, the more he knows that if it's going to get done, he's going to have to do it himself. So he interferes with what they have to do even more.

But Harry knew this when he started.

He could have told you—his new Boss—that ultimately The Boss always interferes.

Harry could have told you that the work will never be done to The Boss's satisfaction.

And the reason is that The Boss always changes his

mind about what needs to be done, and how.

What Harry doesn't know, however, is why—why you're such a madman.

That it's not your people who are driving you crazy.

That it's not the complaining customer who's driving you mad.

That it's not the banker, or the vendor, or the incorrectly wrapped package that's driving you up the wall.

That it's not that "nobody cares," or that "nothing gets done on time" that's driving you insane.

No, it's not the world that's the problem.

It's that you simply don't know how to do it any other way.

You're hopelessly, helplessly at a loss. For you to behave differently you would need to awaken the personalities who have been asleep within you for a long time—The Entrepreneur and The Manager—and then help them to develop the skills only they can add to your business.

But The Technician in you won't stop long enough for that to happen.

The Technician in you has got to go to work!

The Technician in you has got to catch the balls!

The Technician in you has got to keep busy. The Technician in you has just reached the limits of his Comfort Zone.

I looked over at Sarah and could tell I had hit a nerve.

Sarah had discovered something in the course of our conversation—something about her Comfort Zone that was very meaningful for her.

And, intuitively, I knew we had just taken a snapshot of it.

5

BEYOND THE COMFORT ZONE

> Drastic change creates an estrangement from the self,
> and generates a need for a new birth of a new identity.
> And it perhaps depends on the way this need is satis-
> fied whether the process of change runs smoothly or is
> attended with convulsions and explosions.
>
> *Eric Hoffer*
> *The Temper of Our Time*

Every Adolescent business reaches a point where it
pushes beyond its owner's Comfort Zone—the
boundary within which he feels secure in his ability to
control his environment, and outside of which he
begins to lose that control.

The Technician's boundary is determined by how
much he can do himself.

The Manager's is defined by how many technicians
he can supervise effectively or how many subordinate
managers he can organize into a productive effort.

The Entrepreneur's boundary is a function of how
many managers he can engage in pursuit of his vision.

As a business grows, it invariably exceeds its owner's

ability to control it—to touch, feel, and see the work
that needs to be done, and to inspect its progress personally as every technician needs to do.

Out of desperation, he does what he knows how to
do rather than what he doesn't, thereby abdicating his
role as manager and passing his accountability down to
someone else—a "Harry."

At that point, his desperation turns into hope. He
hopes that Harry will handle it so that he won't have to
worry about it anymore.

But Harry has needs of his own. Harry's also a technician. He needs more direction than The Technician
can give him. He needs to know why he's doing what
he's doing. He needs to know the result he's accountable for and the standards against which his work is
being evaluated. He also needs to know where the business is going and where his accountabilities fit into its
overall strategy.

To produce effectively, Harry needs something The
Technician-turned-business-owner isn't capable of giving him—a manager! And the lack of one causes the
business to go into a tailspin.

And as the business grows beyond the owner's Comfort Zone—as the tailspin accelerates—there are only
three courses of action to be taken, only three ways the
business can turn. It can return to Infancy. It can go for
broke. Or it can hang on for dear life.

Let's take a look at each.

Getting Small Again

One of the most consistent and predictable reactions
of The Technician-turned-business-owner to Adolescent

chaos is the decision to "get small" again. If you can't control the chaos, get rid of it.

Go back to the way it used to be when you did everything yourself, when you didn't have people to worry about, or too many customers, or too many unpayable payables and unreceivable receivables, or too much inventory.

In short, go back to the time when business was simple, back to Infancy.

And thousands upon thousands of technicians do just that. They get rid of their people, get rid of their inventory, wrap up their payables in a large bag, rent a smaller facility, put the machine in the middle, put the telephone by the machine, and go back to doing it all by themselves again.

They go back to being the owner, sole proprietor, chief cook and bottle washer—doing everything that needs to be done, all alone, but comfortable with the feeling of regained control.

"What can go wrong?" they think to themselves, forgetting at once that they've been there before. Predictably, this too takes its toll.

One morning—it could be six weeks or six years following the day you "got small" again—the inevitable happens.

You wake up in bed, and your spouse turns to you and says: "What's wrong? You're not looking too good."

"I'm not feeling too good," you answer.

"Do you want to talk about it?" he or she asks.

"It's simple," you say, "I don't want to go in there anymore!"

Then your spouse asks you the obvious question: "But if you don't, who will?"

And all of a sudden you are struck with the reality of your condition.

You realize something you've avoided all these years.

You come face to face with the unavoidable truth:

You don't own a business—you own a job!

What's more, it's the worst job in the world!

You can't close it when you want to, because if it's closed you don't get paid.

You can't leave it when you want to, because when you leave there's nobody there to do the work.

You can't sell it when you want to, because who wants to buy a job?

At that point you feel the despair and the cynicism almost every small business owner gets to feel.

If there was ever a dream, however small, it's gone. And with it, any desire to keep busy, busy, busy.

You don't wash the windows anymore.

You don't sweep the floors.

The customers become a problem rather than an opportunity. Because if somebody buys something, you're going to have to do the work.

Your standards of dress begin to deteriorate.

The sign on the front door fades and peels.

And you don't care.

For when the dream is gone, the only thing left is work.

The tyranny of routine.

The day-to-day grind of purposeless activity.

Finally, you close the doors. There's nothing to keep you there anymore.

According to the Small Business Administration, more than 400,000 such businesses close their doors in the United States every year.

And it's understandable.

Your business, once the shining promise of your life, and now no promise at all, has gradually become a mortuary for dead dreams.

Going for Broke

The Adolescent business has another alternative that is certainly less painful and decidedly more dramatic than "getting small." It can just keep growing faster and faster until it self-destructs of its own momentum.

The roll call is endless: Itel, Osbourne Computer, Coleco, and countless more. All such "going-for-broke" companies were started with an Entrepreneurial Seizure by a Technician who focused on the wrong end of the business, the commodity the business made, rather than the business itself.

"Going-for-broke" businesses are a sign of our time.

They are a high-tech phenomenon.

With the explosion of new technology and the numbers of those who create it, a whole new breed of technicians has flocked to the business arena.

Along with these wizards and their seemingly unlimited technical virtuosity, an avalanche of new products has thundered through the wide-open doors of an enthralled and receptive marketplace.

Unfortunately, most of these companies barely get through the doors before the uncontrollable momentum that got them there forces them to stumble and then fall.

All the excesses of Adolescence, frustrating and bewildering as they might be in a normally expanding company, are disastrous in a "going-for-broke" business.

As quickly as it grows, chaos grows even faster. For tied to the tail of a technological breakthrough, The Technician and his people rarely break free long enough to gain some perspective about their condition. The demand for the commodity of which they are so proud quickly exceeds their chronically Adolescent ability to produce it.

The result is almost always catastrophic. The business explodes, leaving behind it people who most often justify the explosion as an inevitable consequence of doing business on a "fast track" where luck and speed and a brilliant bit of technological daring-do are the necessary components for making it big.

The reality is otherwise.

Luck and speed and brilliant technology have never been enough, because somebody is always luckier, faster, and technologically brighter. Unfortunately, once on a fast track, there's precious little time to listen. The race is won by reflex, a stroke of genius, or a stroke of luck.

"Going for broke" is the high-tech equivalent of Russian Roulette, oftentimes played by people who don't even know the gun is loaded!

Adolescent Survival

The most tragic possibility of all for an Adolescent business is that it actually survives!

You're an incredibly strong-willed, stubborn, single-minded individual who's determined not to be beaten.

You go into your business every morning with a vengeance, absolutely convinced that it's a jungle out there, and fully committed to doing whatever's necessary to survive.

And you do survive. Kicking and scratching, beating up your people and your customers, ranting and raving at your family and friends—because, after all, you've got to keep the business going. And you know there's only one way to do it: *you've got to be there—all the time.*

In Adolescent Survival you're *consumed* by the business and the possibility of losing it.

And so you put everything you have into it.

And, for whatever reason, you manage to keep it going.

Day after day, fighting the same battles, in exactly the same way you did the day before.

You never change.

Night after night, you go home to unwind, only to wind up even tighter in anticipation of tomorrow.

Finally, your business doesn't explode—you do!

You're like a twelve-cylinder engine working on one cylinder, pumping away, trying with everything you've got to produce twelve cylinders worth of results.

But finally, and inevitably, there's nothing left.

There's simply nothing more you can do, except face the fact that one cylinder can't produce the results of twelve, no matter how hard it tries.

Something has to give, and that something is you.

Does this sound familiar?

Well, if you've been in business for a while, it should.

And if you haven't been in business for long, it probably will sound familiar one day.

Because the tragedy is that the condition of Infancy and Adolescence dominates American small business.

It is the condition in most of the small businesses we at E-Myth Worldwide have visited over the past twenty-four years, a condition of rampant confusion and wasted spirits.

It didn't need to happen. There is a better way.

*   *   *

The nerve I had touched earlier in Sarah had diminished enough for her to collect her thoughts.

"How did you know?" she asked me quietly. "Have you been talking to someone about me?" she said, in part wanting to believe I knew more about her story than I had let on, and in part knowing she was just like everyone else.

She knew the answer. Before I could confirm it, she said, "I got small again. And I still don't understand what happened."

She looked around the small shop as though seeing someone or something I couldn't.

"My Harry was Elizabeth," she sighed.

"I hired her when the business was only six months old. She did everything for me, Elizabeth did. She was absolutely incredible. I don't know what I would have done without her. She did the books. She helped me bake. She cleaned up in the morning and after we closed. She hired my first three employees, taught them how to do the various jobs that needed to be done. She was always here when I needed her. And, as the business grew over the next two years, Elizabeth took on more and more of the responsibility for the business. She worked as hard as I did. And she seemed to love it here. And me. She seemed to love me too. Goodness knows, I loved her.

"And then, one day—it was a Wednesday, June 10th, I believe, at seven in the morning—she called me and told me she wouldn't be coming in any longer. That she had taken another job. That she couldn't afford to work for what I was paying her. Just like that! I couldn't believe my ears. I couldn't believe that she meant it. I thought it was a joke. I laughed, and said, 'C'mon Elizabeth,' or something like that. And Elizabeth said she was sorry. And then hung up! Hung up. Just hung up.

"Well, I stood there and wept. And then I felt fear, a fear I hadn't ever felt before. I felt cold inside. How could this be? I thought to myself. How could someone I thought I knew so well, someone I trusted so much, have suddenly become a stranger? What in the world did this say about me? About my lack of judgment? About the conversations I should have had with Elizabeth but didn't?

"But the pies needed to be removed from the oven, and the floors needed to be cleaned, and the shop prepared for opening, and so, despite the pain I was feeling, the sickness in my stomach, I went to work. And I haven't stopped since. The people she hired left soon afterward. To be honest with you, I never really had a connection with them. They were Elizabeth's people.

"When I think back now, I see how easy it was for me to do. How easy it was for me to become absorbed by the work rather than the people. And I guess they knew that. Because after Elizabeth left they all seemed to regard me with suspicion. Like I had let her go without telling them or something. If Elizabeth could leave, a woman like that, what did it say about them for staying? At least that's what I believed they were thinking. Who knew? I was too devastated to ask. Since then I haven't had the heart to hire anyone to replace them. The thought of it is terrifying to me. The thought of bringing strangers into my life like that again feels like a risk I don't want to take. And so I do it all myself. And I know I can't do it much longer. Besides which, what's the point?"

Sarah sighed deeply and looked across at me.

"So, there's my Comfort Zone," she said. "What do I do about that?"

"Start all over again—but differently this time," I answered.

"It's the only way out of the trap."

Most of us have had the experience of being disappointed by someone in whom we have put our trust as a direct result of our indifference or lack of understanding or lack of skill or lack of attention.

And most of us learn eventually, if for no other reason than because we realize that we can't be everywhere at once, to trust again.

But trust can only take us so far.

Trust alone can set us up to repeat those same disappointing experiences.

Because true trust comes from knowing, not from blind faith.

And to know, one must understand.

And to understand, one must have an intimate awareness of what conditions are truly present. What people know and what they don't. What people do and what they don't. What people want and what they don't. How people do what they do and how people don't. Who people are and who they aren't.

In short, Sarah trusted Elizabeth blindly. Sarah simply wanted to believe in Elizabeth. It was easier that way. Because if Sarah trusted blindly, if she simply left it all up to chance, she wouldn't be forced to do the work she didn't want to do. The work of coming to agreement about what her relationship with Elizabeth was about. What role each of them was there to play.

What it meant for Sarah to be an owner and Elizabeth to be her employee. What it meant for Sarah to set out the rules of the game that she was expecting Elizabeth to play.

Because Sarah didn't feel comfortable in this new role, this role of the owner, this role of The Entrepreneur, this role of a businessperson, she left everything up to chance. She abdicated her accountability as an owner and took on the role of just another employee. She avoided fully participating in her relationship with Elizabeth, and, in the process, created a dynamic between herself and her employee built on a weak structure. An omission that foretold Elizabeth's inevitable departure and Sarah's inevitable pain.

I certainly didn't need to tell Sarah that she had no one to blame but herself. I just needed to find the right way to show her how she could do it differently the next time.

"The next time," I said, "you'll know that your business is destined to grow, and that once it does your job is going to be significantly different. For now, that's all you need.

"Small, smaller, smallest. How big is small? One person? Ten people? Sixty people? One hundred fifty people? To a Fortune 500 company, a Fortune 1,000 company is small. To a Fortune 1,000 company, a Fortune 3,000 company is small. To a ten-person company, a two-person company is small.

"The true question is not how small a business should be but how big. How big can your business naturally become, with the operative word being *naturally?*

"Because, whatever that size is, any limitation you place on its growth is unnatural, shaped not by the market or by your lack of capital (even though that may play a part) but by your own personal limitations. Your lack of skill, knowledge, and experience, and, most of all, passion, for growing a healthy, functionally dynamic, extraordinary business.

"In this regard, 'getting small' is, rather than an intentional act, a reaction to the pain and fear induced by uncontrolled and uncontrollable growth, both of which could have been anticipated provided the owner had been prepared to facilitate the growth in a balanced, healthy, proactive way.

"But to do that requires intention at the outset of the business, entrepreneurial intention, as well as a willingness—no, a true passion—for the personal transformation such a process will call for: accessing new skills, new understanding, new knowledge, new emotional depth, new wisdom.

"You might say that the chaos that takes place in every Adolescent business can produce one of two outcomes for the small business owner who suddenly finds himself in the middle of it. For the truly passionate owner, Don Juan's 'warrior,' it can provide him with an opportunity to transmute his personal 'lead' into 'gold.' Or the fires can become so fearsome that he shrinks back to the 'safety' of the smaller life he came from not too long before—the 'lead' I've got is better than the 'gold' I haven't got. Better safe than sorry.

"So, in this context, a business that 'gets small again' is a business reduced to the level of its owner's personal resistance to change, to its owner's Comfort Zone, in which the owner waits and works, works and waits, hoping for something positive to happen.

"This condition reminds me of a line from Samuel

Beckett's *Waiting for Godot* in which Estragon, having waited around for days hoping the mythical Godot will arrive and relieve him of his misery, turns to his companion, Vladimir, and says, 'I can't go on like this.' To which Vladimir replies, 'That's what you think.'

"So, if the natural disposition of every business is to either grow or contract—and it is; there is no denying that—then 'getting small again' is the natural inclination of The Technician-turned-owner to shrink from the unknown, to shrink from the business she has created, to constrain the business from creating demands on her to which she feels hopelessly inadequate to respond appropriately.

"In short, businesses that 'get small again' die. They literally implode upon themselves.

"Not right away, necessarily. But over time they die. Atrophy and die. They can't do anything else.

"And the result of that is enormous disappointment, lost investment, shattered lives, not only the owner's but those of the employees, the families of both the owner and the employees, the customers, the suppliers, the lenders, all of those people whose lives have somehow been intertwined with the life of this small business, and now with its death.

"The tragedy is that all this could have been prevented had the business been started differently, had The Technician suffering from an Entrepreneurial Seizure approached the business in a broader, more entrepreneurial way.

"Of course, you couldn't have anticipated everything that has happened to you so far in your business," I said to Sarah, "but you could have anticipated much of it.

"You could have anticipated what happened to Elizabeth and the people she hired.

"You could have anticipated that people would love your pies and that the business would therefore have to grow.

"You could have anticipated that growth would bring additional responsibilities, additional skills required, additional capital needed to respond to the added demand that growth always places on a business and on people.

"In short, while you couldn't have known everything, you could certainly have known more than you do.

"And that's your job, Sarah! The job of the owner. And if you don't do it, nobody will.

"Simply put, your job is to prepare yourself and your business for growth.

"To educate yourself sufficiently so that, as your business grows, the business's foundation and structure can carry the additional weight.

"And as awesome a responsibility as that may seem to you, you have no other choice—if your business is to thrive, that is.

"It's up to you to dictate your business's rate of growth as best you can by understanding the key processes that need to be performed, the key objectives that need to be achieved, the key position you are aiming your business to hold in the marketplace.

"By asking the right questions, such as: Where do I wish to be? When do I wish to be there? How much capital will that take? How many people, doing what work, and how? What technology will be required? How large a space will be needed, at Benchmark One, at Benchmark Two, at Benchmark Three?

"Will you be wrong at times? Will you make mistakes? Will you change your mind? Of course you will! More often than not. But, done right, you will also have contingency plans in place. Best case, worst case. And sometimes you will simply fly by the seat of your pants; you will go with the flow, follow your intuition.

"But all the while, even while you're guessing, the key is to plan, envision, and articulate what you see in the future both for yourself and for your employees. Because if you don't articulate it—I mean, write it down, clearly, so others can understand it—you don't own it! And do you know that in all the years I've been doing this work with small business owners, out of the thousands upon thousands we've met, there have only been a few who had any plan at all! Nothing written, nothing committed to paper, nothing concrete at all.

"Remember, Sarah, any plan is better than no plan.

"Because in the process of defining the future, the plan begins to shape itself to reality, both the reality of the world out there and the reality you are able to create in here.

"And as those two realities merge, they form a new reality—call it your reality, call it the unique invention that is uniquely yours, the reality of your mind and your heart uniting with all the elements of your business, and your business with the world, shaping, designing, collaborating, to form something that never existed before in exactly that way.

"And that is the sign of a Mature company. A Mature company is started differently than all the rest. A Mature company is founded on a broader perspective, an entrepreneurial perspective, a more intelligent point of view. About building a business that works not because of you but without you.

"And because it starts that way, it is more likely to

continue that way. And therein resides the true difference between an Adolescent company, where everything is left up to chance, and a Mature company, where
there is a vision against which the present is shaped.

"But I'm getting ahead of myself," I said. "The
important thing is that your experience could have been
completely different. That there is an entirely different
way to start a business than the way you and most
Technicians-turned-business-owners start theirs. And
that anyone can do it!"

I looked at Sarah and caught the glow in her eyes.

"I'm inspired by the idea of it," she said softly. "All
of a sudden everything that has looked so dark feels
light again."

But, no sooner had she begun to let herself thrill to
the idea of building a business that works that some
other thought—a dark thought—captured her attention.

"But what do I do about Elizabeth?" she said.

"What do I do about Elizabeth?" The question every
Technician-turned-owner wants answered.

As though, by answering that question, everything
else will be answered.

As if the answer to all of the frustrations most small
business owners experience is somehow tied to particular people.

As if within the complexity of Sarah's relationship
with Elizabeth—within all relationships for that matter—there exists some key which, once turned, could
make everything right again.

Well, I'm no genius, but I know that there is no such
key.

There's just us, you and me, fumbling about in our

often inadequate way, constantly being surprised by our own and other people's behavior, how badly we've done it, how out of touch with our own and others' feelings we've discovered ourselves to be.

I looked Sarah in the eye, got very quiet, and said, "Sarah, the real question is not what to do about Elizabeth but what do you do about all the Elizabeths in your future?

"You did the best you could. And so did Elizabeth. It's time to get on with your life. To build your business in an enlivening way. Are you ready?"

Sarah smiled at me, her eyes positively gleaming.

"I'm ready if you are," she said.

"Then let's talk about Maturity for a minute," I said. "Because that's where your future lies."

6

MATURITY AND THE ENTREPRENEURIAL PERSPECTIVE

They see the pattern, understand the order, experience
the vision.

Peter Drucker
The New Society

Maturity, the third phase of a company's growth, is
exemplified by the best businesses in the world.
Businesses such as McDonald's, Federal Express, and
Disney.

A Mature business knows how it got to be where it
is, and what it must do to get where it wants to go.

Therefore, Maturity is not an inevitable result of the
first two phases. It is not the end product of a serial process, beginning with Infancy and moving through Adolescence.

No, companies like McDonald's, Federal Express,
and Disney didn't end up as Mature companies. They
started out that way! The people who started them had
a totally different perspective about what a business is
and why it works.

The person who launches his business as a Mature company must also go through Infancy and Adolescence. He simply goes through them in an entirely different way.

It's his *perspective* that makes the difference.

His Entrepreneurial Perspective.

The Entrepreneurial Perspective

I once heard a story about Tom Watson, the founder of IBM. Asked to what he attributed the phenomenal success of IBM, he is said to have answered:

IBM is what it is today for three special reasons. The first reason is that, at the very beginning, I had a very clear picture of what the company would look like when it was finally done. You might say I had a model in my mind of what it would look like when the dream—my vision—was in place.

The second reason was that once I had that picture, I then asked myself how a company which looked like that would have to act. I then created a picture of how IBM would act when it was finally done.

The third reason IBM has been so successful was that once I had a picture of how IBM would look when the dream was in place and how such a company would have to act, I then realized that, unless we began to act that way from the very beginning, we would never get there.

In other words, I realized that for IBM to become a great company it would have to act like a great company long before it ever became one.

From the very outset, IBM was fashioned after the template of my vision. And each and every day we attempted to model the company after that template. At the end of each day, we asked ourselves how well we did, discovered the disparity between where we were and where we had committed ourselves to be, and, at the start of the following day, set out to make up for the difference.

Every day at IBM was a day devoted to business development, not doing business.

We didn't do business at IBM, we built one

Now, it's been more than thirty years since Tom Watson Sr. spoke about the reasons for IBM's success and I recognize what people might say about this $88.4 billion company. That it's a business in trouble. That it's lost its way. That it's hardly an exemplar for any business owner to follow. But if Watson were alive today, I'm certain it would be different. I'm certain that the entrepreneurial genius that gave rise to IBM would, if it were present today—and I don't know that it isn't, but all the signs are there—be engaged in the reinvention of the company as surely as it had been reinvented time and time again, to re-create its future as the future demanded.

In short, my storyteller may not have had Watson's words exactly verbatim, but what the story tells us is very important.

It reveals an understanding of what makes a great business great.

It also tells us what makes all other businesses survivable at their best; intolerable at their worst.

It tells us that the very best businesses are fashioned after a model of a business that works.

It tells us that it is the Entrepreneurial Perspective that says it's not the commodity or the work itself that is important. What's important is the business: how it looks, how it acts, how it does what it is intended to do.

It says that Tom Watson Sr. had a passion for the enterprise itself.

And that, unfortunately, most people who go into business don't.

That most people who go into business don't have a model of a business that works, but of work itself, a Technician's Perspective, which differs from the Entrepreneurial Perspective in the following ways:

- The Entrepreneurial Perspective asks the question: "How must the business work?" The Technician's Perspective asks: "What work has to be done?"
- The Entrepreneurial Perspective sees the business as a system for producing outside results—for the customer—resulting in profits. The Technician's Perspective sees the business as a place in which people work to produce inside results—for The Technician—producing income.
- The Entrepreneurial Perspective starts with a picture of a well-defined future, and then comes back to the present with the intention of changing it to match the vision. The Technician's Perspective starts with the present, and then looks forward to an uncertain future with the hope of keeping it much like the present.
- The Entrepreneurial Perspective envisions the business in its entirety, from which is derived its parts. The Technician's Perspective envisions the business in parts, from which is constructed the whole.
- The Entrepreneurial Perspective is an integrated

vision of the world. The Technician's Perspective
is a fragmented vision of the world.

- To The Entrepreneur, the present-day world is
  modeled after his vision. To The Technician, the
  future is modeled after the present-day world.

Is it any wonder that the Entrepreneurial Perspective
is absolutely necessary for the creation of a great business, while The Technician's produces its exact opposite?

The Entrepreneurial Perspective adopts a wider, more
expansive scale. It views the business as a network of
seamlessly integrated components, each contributing to
some larger pattern that comes together in such a way
as to produce a specifically planned result, a systematic
way of doing business.

Each step in the development of such a business is
measurable, if not quantitatively, at least, qualitatively.
There's a standard for the business, a form, a way of
being that can be translated into things to do today that
best exemplify it. The business operates according to
articulated rules and principles. It has a clear, recogniz-
able form.

With The Technician's Perspective, however, the
scale is narrower, more inhibited, confined principally
to the work being done.

As a result, The Technician's business becomes
increasingly oppressive, less exhilarating, closed off
from the larger world outside.

His business is reduced to steps that fail to take him
anywhere other than to the next step, itself nothing
more than a replica of the one before it.

Routine becomes the order of the day.

Work is done for work's sake alone, forsaking any higher purpose, any meaning for what needs to be done other than the need to just do it.

The Technician sees no connection between where his business is going and where it is now.

Lacking the grander scale and visionary guidance manifest in the Entrepreneurial Model, The Technician is left to construct a model each step of the way.

But the only model from which to construct it is the model of past experience, the model of work. Exactly the opposite of what he needs if the business is to free him of the work he's grown accustomed to doing.

The Entrepreneurial Model

What does The Entrepreneur see off in the distance that The Technician finds so difficult to see? What exactly is the Entrepreneurial Model?

It's a model of a business that fulfills the perceived needs of a specific segment of customers in an innovative way.

The Entrepreneurial Model looks at a business as if it were a product, sitting on a shelf and competing for the customer's attention against a whole shelf of competing products (or businesses).

Said another way, the Entrepreneurial Model has less to do with what's done in a business and more to do with how it's done. The commodity isn't what's important—the way it's delivered is.

When The Entrepreneur creates the model, he surveys the world and asks: "Where is the opportunity?" Having identified it, he then goes back to the drawing board and constructs a solution to the frustrations he finds among a certain group of customers. A solution in the form of a business that looks and acts in a very specific way, the way the customer needs it to look and act, not The Entrepreneur.

"How will my business look to the customer?" The Entrepreneur asks. "How will my business stand out from all the rest?"

Thus, the Entrepreneurial Model does not start with a picture of the business to be created but of the customer for whom the business is to be created.

It understands that *without a clear picture of that customer, no business can succeed.*

The Technician, on the other hand, looks inwardly, to define his skills, and only looks outwardly afterward to ask, "How can I sell them?"

The resulting business almost inevitably focuses on the thing it sells rather than the way the business goes about it or the customer to whom it's to be sold.

Such a business is designed to satisfy The Technician who created it, not the customer.

To The Entrepreneur, the business is the product.

To The Technician, the product is what he delivers to the customer.

To The Technician, the customer is always a problem. Because the customer never seems to want what The Technician has to offer at the price at which he offers it.

To The Entrepreneur, however, the customer is always an opportunity. Because The Entrepreneur knows that within the customer is a continuing parade of changing wants begging to be satisfied. All The Entrepreneur has to do is find out what those wants are and what they will be in the future.

As a result, the world is a continuing surprise, a treasure hunt to The Entrepreneur.

To The Technician, however, the world is a place that never seems to let him do what he wants to do; it rarely applauds his efforts; it rarely appreciates his work; it rarely, if ever, appreciates him. To The Technician, the world always wants something he doesn't know how to give it.

The question then becomes, how can we introduce the entrepreneurial model to The Technician in such a way that he can understand it and utilize it?

The answer is, unfortunately, we can't.

The Technician isn't interested.

The Technician has other things to do.

If we are to be successful at this, what we must do, instead, is to give the undeveloped Entrepreneur in each of us the information he needs to grow beyond the limitations of The Technician's Comfort Zone so as to experience a vision of a business that works.

What we must do, instead, is to provide our inner entrepreneur with a model of a business that works, a model that is so exciting that it stimulates our entrepreneurial personality—our innovative side—to break free of The Technician's bonds once and for all.

What we must do, instead, is discover a model that sparks the entrepreneurial imagination in each of us with such a resounding shock that by the time The Technician wakes up to the fact it will be too late, The Entrepreneur will be well on his way.

But, at the same time, if the model is to work, if the model is to awaken The Entrepreneur within each of us to begin to rebuild our businesses around the Entrepreneurial Perspective they so desperately need to flourish, The Manager and The Technician need their own models.

Because if The Entrepreneur drives the business, The Manager must make certain it has the necessary fuel for sustenance, and that the engine and chassis are in a good state of repair.

If The Technician is to be satisfied, on the other hand, there must be a model that provides him with work that satisfies his need for direct interaction with every nut and bolt.

In short, for this business model of ours to work, it must be balanced and inclusive so that The Entrepreneur, The Manager, and The Technician all find their natural place within it, so that they all find the right work to do.

To find such a model, let us examine a revolutionary development that has transformed American small business in an astonishing way.

I call it the Turn-Key Revolution.

It was time for Sarah to open her store. And we still had a lot of work to do.

"I'll come back tonight," I said. "Can I answer any questions before I leave?"

"Yes," Sarah smiled. "How soon can we get started?"

PART II

The Turn-Key Revolution: A New View of Business

7

THE TURN-KEY REVOLUTION

Systems theory looks at the world in terms of the interrelatedness of all phenomena, and in this framework an integrated whole whose properties cannot be reduced to those of its parts is called a system.

Fritjof Capra
The Turning Point

The Industrial Revolution, the Technological Revolution, the Information Explosion are all familiar phenomena in today's world. There is no question of the impact each has had on our lives.

If asked to describe the Turn-Key Revolution, however, most people would simply respond with a blank stare.

Yet the impact of the Turn-Key Revolution on American small business, and the inferences we can draw about that impact for the future, are as profound as any of the phenomena cited above.

For at the heart of the Turn-Key Revolution is a way of doing business that has the power to dramatically transform any small business—indeed, any business, no matter what its size—from a condition of chaos and disease to a condition of order, excitement, and continuous growth. It is the Turn-Key Revolution that provides us with that illusive key to the development of an extraordinary business: the ultimately balanced model of a business that works.

The Franchise Phenomenon

It all started in 1952 when a fifty-two-year-old salesman walked into a hamburger stand in San Bernardino, California, to sell the two brothers who owned it a milkshake machine.

What he saw there was a miracle.

At least that's how Ray Kroc, the milkshake machine salesman, might have described it. For he had never seen anything like that very first MacDonald's (later to become McDonald's) hamburger stand.

It worked like a Swiss watch!

Hamburgers were produced in a way he'd never seen before—quickly, efficiently, inexpensively, and identically.

Best of all, anyone could do it.

He watched high school kids working with precision under the supervision of the owners, happily responding to the long lines of customers queued up in front of the stand.

It became apparent to Ray Kroc that what the MacDonald brothers had created was not just another hamburger stand but a money machine!

Soon after that first visit, and possessed by a passion he had never felt quite like that before, Ray Kroc convinced Mac and Jim MacDonald to let him franchise their method.

Twelve years and several million hamburgers later, he bought them out and went on to create the largest retail prepared food distribution system in the world.

"The Most Successful Small Business in the World"

That's what McDonald's calls itself today.

And for good reason.

Because the success of McDonald's is truly staggering.

Think about it. In less than forty years, Ray Kroc's McDonald's has become a $40-billion-a-year business, with 28,707 restaurants worldwide—and growing in number every minute—serving food to more than 43 million people every day in 120 countries, representing more than 10 percent of the gross restaurant receipts in America!

The average McDonald's restaurant produces more than $2 million in annual sales, and is more profitable than almost any other retail business in the world, with an average 17 percent pretax net profit.

But Ray Kroc created much more than just a fantastically successful business. He created the model upon which an entire generation of entrepreneurs have since built their fortunes—a model that was the genesis of the franchise phenomenon.

It started as a trickle when a few entrepreneurs began to experiment with Kroc's formula for success. But it wasn't long before the trickle turned into Niagara Falls!

In 2000, there were 320,000 franchised businesses in 75 industries. Franchises produce $1-trillion in sales each year—almost 50 percent of every retail dollar spent in the nation—and had more than 8 million full- and part-time people, the largest employer of high school youth in the country's economy.

But the genius of McDonald's isn't franchising it-self. The franchise has been around for more than a hundred years. Many companies—Coca-Cola and General Motors among them—have utilized franchising as an effective method of distribution to reach broadly expanding markets inexpensively. The true genius of Ray Kroc's McDonald's is the Business Format Franchise.

It is the Business Format Franchise that has revolutionized American business.

It is the Business Format Franchise, with one new franchise opening its doors every eight minutes of every single business day, that has spawned so much of the success of the franchise phenomenon over the past forty years.

And, according to studies conducted by the U.S. Commerce Department from 1971 to 1987, less than 5 percent of franchises have been terminated on an annual basis, or 25 percent in five years.

Compare that statistic to the more than 80-percent failure rate of independently owned businesses, and you can immediately understand the power of the Turn-Key Revolution in our economy, and the contribution that the Business Format Franchise has made to it and the future success of your business.

Turning the Key: The Business Format Franchise

The early franchise businesses, many of which still exist, were called "trade name" franchises.

Under this system, the franchisor licenses the right to small companies to market its nationally known products locally.

But the Business Format Franchise moves a step beyond the trade name franchise.

The Business Format Franchise not only lends its name to the smaller enterprise but it also *provides the franchisee with an entire system of doing business.*

And in that difference lies the true significance of the Turn-Key Revolution and its phenomenal success.

The Turn-Key Revolution and the Business Format Franchise were born of a belief that runs counter to what most business founders in this country believe.

Most business founders believe that the success of a business resides in the success of the product it sells.

To the trade name franchisor, the value of the franchise lies in the value of the brand name that it is licensing: Cadillac, Mercedes, Coca-Cola.

There was a time when that belief was true, but it isn't anymore. In a world where brand names proliferate like snowflakes in a Minnesota blizzard, it becomes more and more difficult—and infinitely more expensive—to establish a secure position with a brand name and expect to keep it.

As a result, trade name franchises have been declining over the same period that franchising in general has been exploding at an unprecedented rate.

It is the Business Format Franchise that has accounted for that growth.

Because the Business Format Franchise is built on the belief that the true product of a business is not what it sells but how it sells it.

The true product of a business is the business itself.

What Ray Kroc understood at McDonald's was that the hamburger wasn't his product. *McDonald's was.* And he believed that for a most important reason.

Selling the Business Instead of the Product

Ray Kroc was the consummate entrepreneur. And like most entrepreneurs, he suffered from one major liability. He had a huge dream and very little money.

Enter the franchisee.

The franchisee became the vehicle for Ray Kroc to realize his dream.

At that point, Ray Kroc began to look at his business as the product, and at the franchisee as his first, last, and most important customer.

For the franchisee wasn't interested in hamburgers or french fries or milkshakes; he was interested in the business.

Driven by his desire to buy a business, the franchisee only wanted to know one thing: "Does it work?"

Ray Kroc's most important concern then became how to make certain his business would work better than any other.

If McDonald's was to fulfill the dream he had for it, the franchisee would have to be willing to buy it.

And the only way Ray Kroc could assure himself of that was to make certain that McDonald's worked better than any of the other business products around.

At the outset, Ray Kroc wasn't just competing with other hamburger businesses—he was competing with every other business opportunity around!

But there was a second reason that Ray Kroc had for making certain McDonald's would work.

Given the failure rate of most small businesses, he must have realized a crucial fact: for McDonald's to be a predictable success, the business would have to work, because the franchisee, if left to his own devices, most assuredly wouldn't!

Once he understood this, Ray Kroc's problem became his opportunity.

Forced to create a business that worked in order to sell it, he also created a business that would work once it was sold, no matter who bought it.

Armed with that realization, he set about the task of creating a foolproof, predictable business.

A systems-dependent business, not a people-dependent business.

A business that could work without him.

Unlike most small business owners before him—and since—Ray Kroc went to work *on* his business, not *in* it.

He began to think about his business like an engineer working on a pre-production prototype of a mass-produceable product.

He began to *reengineer* McDonald's decades before the word and the process came into fashion.

He began to think about McDonald's just like Henry Ford must have thought about the Model T.

How could the components of the prototype be constructed so that it could be assembled at a very low cost with totally interchangeable parts?

How could the components be constructed so that the resulting business system could be replicated over and over again, each business working—just like the Model T—as reliably as the thousands that preceded it?

What Ray Kroc did was to apply the thinking behind the Industrial Revolution to the process of Business

Development, and to a degree never before experienced in a business enterprise.

The business-as-a-product would only sell if it worked. And the only way to make certain it would work in the hands of a franchisee anywhere in the world would be to build it out of perfectly predictable components that could be tested in a prototype long before ever going into mass production.

Therein lies the secret behind the stunning success of the Business Format Franchise, the launching pad for the Turn-Key Revolution.

That secret is the Franchise Prototype.

It is in the Franchise Prototype that every successful franchisor builds his future.

It is in the Franchise Prototype that every extraordinary franchisor plants the seeds of his fortune.

And it is in the Franchise Prototype that you can find the model you need to make your business work.

Sarah and I couldn't have picked a better time to have this conversation.

If she had ever felt the weight of being a Technician-turned-business-owner, caught up in the doing of her business and the inordinate price she was paying for it, it was right now.

It was ten o'clock at night. As usual, she had had a tumultuous day. Her face was flush with the exertion of mopping the floors, bundling and tossing out the trash, preparing the ovens for the next day, cleaning the counters to their original high luster—in addition to a full day of waiting on customers; serving up pie, coffee, and tea; washing, drying, and stacking plates, cups, saucers; and shining the silver.

And yet, with all that had gone on in the shop that day, you couldn't have known it; for, as always, the shop was impeccable. And, despite the cost to her of keeping it that way, I couldn't help but notice the deep satisfaction Sarah felt as she surveyed her domain. But she was obviously tired.

We pulled two chairs up to a table and quietly sipped the tea she had prepared for us. The large clock ticked emphatically on the wall, punctuating our silence. An occasional car drove by the shop. People walked by the shop's windows, occasionally looking into the shop as they continued on their journey into the night.

I waited for a sign from Sarah that she was ready.

Finally, she began thoughtfully and quietly. "You talk about McDonald's as an example to be modeled. I'm not sure I agree with you about that. I know if my aunt were here today, she would think of McDonald's as exactly the opposite of what you've suggested it is. Talk to me about that," she said. "I'm interested in how you would respond to my aunt, about what you would say to her."

"You know, Sarah," I began, "I can sense that something has shifted in you today. Something important. I can sense also from the tone of your question that you're truly interested in pursuing this question about McDonald's, and I'm inspired to engage in the question with you at the deepest level. I want to thank you for that.

"It's true, many small business owners at first misunderstand my point about McDonald's. They associate fast food with low quality. They infer, then, that by setting McDonald's up as an example, I'm suggesting that one can be incredibly successful in business despite the seemingly low quality of the product delivered. When exactly the opposite is true. But, let me get back to that in a moment.

"As for your aunt, even though I have never met her, from the way you have described her I feel I know her. And this is what I would say to her if she were here asking me the question herself:

"I would say that Ray Kroc was a man with a purpose. His purpose was clear, undiluted, and sure. He lived in an ordinary world, like we all do, a world in which most things didn't work the way they were supposed to. At McDonald's, he saw something that did work, exactly as it was supposed to, time after time after time. To Ray Kroc, that was an inspiration. In fact, he was awed by it. He was a simple man. And he fell in love with the sheer enormity of the thing he called McDonald's.

"As certainly as you loved baking pies, Ray Kroc loved making McDonald's. As certainly as you loved producing an exceptional pie, Ray Kroc loved producing an exceptional result, the same way, with the same impact, time after time. As certainly as you loved the aroma, the smells, the sight, the taste, of your kitchen, Ray Kroc loved the aroma, the smells, the sight, the taste of McDonald's. He was a man in love.

"Now, from the outside in, I can understand why you might be critical of McDonald's. You might say that people shouldn't eat meat. You might say that the hamburgers could be fatter, or less fatty, or this or that. But what you couldn't say—what you could never say— is that McDonald's doesn't keep its promise. Because it does. Better than just about any business in the world, McDonald's, the love of Ray Kroc's life, still keeps its promise, long after Ray Kroc has gone. It delivers exactly what we have come to expect of it every single time.

"So that's why I look upon McDonald's as a model for every small business.

"Because it can do in its more than 28,000 stores what most of us can't do in one!

"And to me, that's what integrity is all about. It's about doing what you say you will do, and, if you can't, learning how.

"If that is the measure of an incredible business— and I believe it is—then there is no more incredible business than McDonald's. Who among us small business owners can say we do things as well?

"But McDonald's is even more important than that.

"McDonald's has not only created an extraordinary business, it has created for all of us small business owners an extraordinary way to create an extraordinary business. It has created a model we can emulate.

"And the profound impact that that has had on our economy over the past four decades is beyond our comprehension.

"So, Sarah's aunt, I honestly believe if you had known Ray Kroc, you would have discovered in him a kindred spirit.

"You would have invited him into your kitchen and he would have invited you into his.

"You would have discussed with him with great passion the art of creating a fine pie crust and he would have discussed with you—with just as great a passion— the art of creating a fine french fry.

"You would have shared with him your secret for preparing the fruit, just as he would share with you his secret for preparing the hamburger buns he so lovingly devoted himself to.

"You are two peas in a pod with one big exception.

"You, Sarah's aunt, had but one kitchen in which you loved to work, your kitchen, making your pies, alone, or with Sarah by your side.

"Ray Kroc had thousands of kitchens, in which he loved to work, perfecting all the time his ability to touch millions of people with the same loving attention you've lavished on a few.

"You are a Technician, a craftsperson, who loves what you do.

"He was an Entrepreneur, albeit still a craftsperson, who loved what he did.

"The only difference between the two of you is an order of magnitude.

"So let me tell you how he crafted something that size."

8

THE FRANCHISE PROTOTYPE

Precision instruments are designed to achieve an idea,
dimensional precision, where perfection is impossible.
There is no perfectly shaped part of the motorcycle and
never will be, but when you come as close as these
instruments take you, remarkable things happen, and
you go flying across the countryside under a power
that would be called magic if it were not so completely
rational in every way.

Robert M. Pirsig
Zen and the Art of Motorcycle Maintenance

The success of the Business Format Franchise is
without question the most important news in business.

Over the course of one year, Business Format Franchises have reported a success rate of 95 percent in
contrast to the 50-plus-percent failure rate of new
independently owned businesses. Where 80 percent of
all businesses fail in the first five years, 75 percent of
all Business Format Franchises succeed!

The reason for that success is the Franchise Prototype.

To the franchisor, the Prototype becomes the working

model of the dream; it is the dream in microcosm. The Prototype becomes the incubator and the nursery for all creative thought, the station where creativity is nursed by pragmatism to grow into an innovation that works.

The Franchise Prototype is also the place where all assumptions are put to the test to see how well they work before becoming operational in the business.

Without it the franchise would be an impossible dream, as chaotic and undisciplined as any business.

The Prototype acts as a buffer between hypothesis and action. Putting ideas to the test in the *real* world rather than the world of competing ideas. The only criterion of value becomes the answer to the ultimate question: "Does it work?"

Once having completed his Prototype, the franchisor then turns to the franchisee and says, "Let me show you how it works."

And work it does. The system runs the business. The people run the system.

In the Franchise Prototype, the system becomes the solution to the problems that have beset all businesses and all human organizations since time immemorial.

The system integrates all the elements required to make a business work. It transforms a business into a machine, or more accurately, because it is so alive, into an organism, driven by the integrity of its parts, all working in concert toward a realized objective. And, with its Prototype as its progenitor, it works like nothing else before it.

At Ray Kroc's McDonald's, every possible detail of the business system was first tested in the Prototype, and then controlled to a degree never before possible in a people-intensive business.

The french fries were left in the warming bin for no more than seven minutes to prevent sogginess. A soggy french fry is not a McDonald's french fry.

Hamburgers were removed from the hot trays in no more than ten minutes to retain the proper moisture.

The frozen meat patties, precisely identical in size and weight, were turned at exactly the same time on the griddle.

Pickles were placed by hand in a set pattern that prevented them from sliding out and landing in the customer's lap.

Food was served to the customer in sixty seconds or less.

Discipline, standardization, and order were the watchwords.

Cleanliness was enforced with meticulous attention to the most seemingly trivial detail.

Ray Kroc was determined that the customer would not equate *inexpensive* with *inattentive or cheap.* Nowhere had a business ever paid so much attention to the little things, to the system that guaranteed the customer that her expectations would be fulfilled in exactly the same way every time.

Unlike the trade name franchise before it, Ray Kroc's system left the franchisee with as little operating discretion as possible.

This was accomplished by sending him through a rigorous training program before ever being allowed to operate the franchise.

At McDonald's, they called it the University of Hamburgerology, or Hamburger U.

There, the franchisee learned not how to make hamburgers but how to run the system that makes hamburgers—the system by which McDonald's satisfied its customers every single time. The system that was to be the foundation of McDonald's uncommon success.

Is it any wonder that McDonald's calls itself "The Most Successful Small Business In The World!"

It is!

Every single extraordinary detail Ray Kroc invented four decades ago is even more extraordinary today.

Whether it is Hamburger U, or the placement of pickles, or the exacting way in which the buns are warmed before serving, or the thickness of the patty— all of it, today, long after Ray Kroc has gone, is still known by the franchisee as the system at the heart of McDonald's.

And just as it was then, it is now. Once the franchisee learns the system, he is given the key to his own business.

Thus, the name: Turn-Key Operation.

The franchisee is licensed the right to use the system, learns how to run it, and then "turns the key." The business does the rest.

And the franchisees love it!

Because if the franchisor has designed the business well, every problem has been thought through. All that's left for the franchisee to do is learn how to manage the system.

That's what the Franchise Prototype is all about.

It's a place to conceive and perfect the system. To find out what works because you've worked it.

The system isn't something you bring to the business. It's something you derive from the process of building the business.

The Franchise Prototype is the answer to the perpetual question: "How do I give my customer what he wants while maintaining control of the business that's giving it to him?"

To The Entrepreneur, the Franchise Prototype is the medium through which his vision takes form in the real world.

To The Manager, the Franchise Prototype provides the order, the predictability, the system so important to his life.

To The Technician, the Prototype is a place in which he is free to do the things he loves to do—technical work.

And to the small business owner, the Franchise Prototype provides the means through which he can finally feed his three personalities in a balanced way while creating a business that works.

So, now you have it: the Franchise Prototype is the model you've been looking for. The Franchise Prototype is the model of a business that works. The balanced model that will satisfy The Entrepreneur, The Manager, and The Technician all at once.

And it's been there all the time!

It's been there at McDonald's. And at Federal Express. And at Disney World. And at Mrs. Field's Cookies.

It's been there at Subway Sandwiches and Domino's Pizza and Kentucky Fried Chicken and Pizza Hut.

It's been there at Taco Bell and UPS and Universal Studios.

It's been there, waiting for you to discover it, all this time!

It's been there in the form of a Proprietary Operating System at the heart of every extraordinary business around you, franchised or not.

Because, after all, that's all that any Business Format Franchise really is.

It is a proprietary way of doing business that successfully and preferentially differentiates every extraordinary business from every one of its competitors. In this light, every great business in the world is a franchise.

The question is: How do you build yours? How do you put this powerfully liberating idea to work for you?

How do you create your Franchise Prototype?

How do you, like Ray Kroc, build a business that works predictably, effortlessly, and profitably each and every day?

How do you build a business that works without you?

How do you get free of your business to live a fuller life?

Do you get it? Do you see why this is so important?

Because until you do it, your business will control your life!

But once you begin to put this idea to work for you, you're on the way to being free!

I could see that Sarah got it.

I could see that the flush on her cheeks now had nothing to do with the work she'd been doing all day.

I could see that her dark, intelligent, creative eyes were riveted on mine, and that the questions were bubbling within her. She was feeling excitement contemplating the creation of an entrepreneurial business.

And she knew she had one already.

She could do in her business what Ray Kroc had done in his. All she needed to do was learn how!

9

WORKING *ON* YOUR BUSINESS, NOT *IN* IT

> ... form is only a beginning. It is the combination of feelings and a function; shapes and things that come to one in connection with the discoveries made as one goes into the wood that pull it together and give meaning to form.
>
> *James Krenov*
> *A Cabinetmaker's Notebook*

It is critical that you understand the point I'm about to make. For if you do, neither your business nor your life will ever be the same.

The point is: *your business is not your life.*

Your business and your life are two totally separate things.

At its best, your business is something apart from you, rather than a part of you, with its own rules and its own purposes. An organism, you might say, that will live or die according to how well it performs its sole function: to find and keep customers.

Once you recognize that the purpose of your life is

not to serve your business, but that the primary purpose of your business is to serve your life, you can then go to work *on* your business, rather than *in* it, with a full understanding of why it is absolutely necessary for you to do so.

This is where you can put the model of the Franchise Prototype to work for you.

Where working *on* your business rather than *in* your business will become the central theme of your daily activity, the prime catalyst for everything you do from this moment forward.

Pretend that the business you own—or want to own—is the prototype, or will be the prototype, for 5,000 more just like it.

That your business is going to serve as the model for 5,000 more just like it.

Not *almost* like it, but *just* like it. Perfect replicates. Clones.

In other words, pretend that you are going to franchise your business. (Note: I said *pretend*. I'm not saying that you should. That isn't the point here—unless, of course, you want it to be.)

Further, now that you know what the game is —the franchise game—understand that there are rules to follow if you are to win:

1. The model will provide consistent value to your customers, employees, suppliers, and lenders, beyond what they expect.
2. The model will be operated by people with the lowest possible level of skill.
3. The model will stand out as a place of impeccable order.

4. All work in the model will be documented in Operations Manuals.
5. The model will provide a uniformly predictable service to the customer.
6. The model will utilize a uniform color, dress, and facilities code.

Let's take a look at each of these rules in turn.

1. The Model Will Provide Consistent Value to Your Customers, Employees, Suppliers, and Lenders, Beyond What They Expect

What is value?

How do we understand it? I would suggest that *value* is what people perceive it to be, and nothing more.

So what could your Prototype do that would not only provide consistent value to your customers, employees, suppliers, and lenders but would provide it beyond their wildest expectations?

That is the question every Entrepreneur must ask.

Because it is the raison d'être of his business!

It is in the understanding of value, as it impacts every person with whom your business comes into contact, that every extraordinary business lives.

Value can be a word said at the door of the business as a customer leaves.

Value can be an unexpected gift from the business arriving in the mail.

Value can be a word of recognition to a new recruit for a job well done, or, for that matter, to a seasoned salesperson who's been successful for years.

Value can be the reasonable price of your products, or the dedication you show in the process of explaining them to a customer who needs more help than usual.

Value can be a simple word of thanks to your banker for his conscientiousness.

Value is essential to your business and to the satisfaction you get from it as it grows.

2. The Model Will Be Operated by People with the Lowest Possible Level of Skill

Yes, I said *lowest* possible level of skill. Because if your model depends on highly skilled people, it's going to be impossible to replicate. Such people are at a premium in the marketplace. They're also expensive, thus raising the price you will have to charge for your product or service.

By lowest possible level of skill I mean the lowest possible level necessary to fulfill the functions for which each is intended. Obviously, if yours is a legal firm, you must have attorneys. If yours is a medical firm, you must have physicians. But you don't need to hire brilliant attorneys or brilliant physicians. You need to create the very best system through which good attorneys and good physicians can be leveraged to produce exquisite results.

The question you need to keep asking yourself is: How can I give my customer the results he wants systematically rather than personally? Put another way: How can I create a business whose results are *systems*-dependent rather than *people*-dependent? *Systems*-dependent rather than *expert*-dependent.

How can I create an expert system rather than hire one?

That is not to say that people are unimportant. On the contrary, people bring systems to life.

People make it possible for things that are designed to work to produce the intended results. And, in the process, people who are systems oriented—as all your people must be—learn how to more effectively make things work for your customers and for your business by learning how to improve the systems.

It's been said, and I believe it to be true, that great businesses are not built by extraordinary people but by ordinary people doing extraordinary things.

But for ordinary people to do extraordinary things, a system—"a way of doing things"—is absolutely essential in order to compensate for the disparity between the skills your people have and the skills your business needs if it is to produce consistent results.

In this context, the system becomes the tools your people use to increase their productivity, to get the job done in the way it needs to get done in order for your business to successfully differentiate itself from your competition.

It's your job—more accurately, the job of your business—to develop those tools and to teach your people how to use them.

It's your people's job to use the tools you've developed and to recommend improvements based on their experience with them.

There's another reason for this rule—what I call the Rule of Ordinary People—that says the blessing of ordinary people is that they make your job *more difficult.*

The typical owner of a small business prefers highly skilled people because he believes they make his job easier—he can simply leave the work to them.

That is, the typical small business owner prefers Management by Abdication to Management by Delegation.

Unfortunately, the inevitable result of this kind of thinking is that the business also grows to depend on the whims and moods of its people.

If they're in the mood, the job gets done.

If they're not, it doesn't.

In this kind of business, a business that relies on discretion, "How do I motivate my people?" becomes the constant question. "How do I keep them in the mood?"

It is literally impossible to produce a consistent result in a business that depends on extraordinary people. No business can do it for long. And no extraordinary business tries to!

Because every extraordinary business knows that when you intentionally build your business around the skills of ordinary people, you will be forced to ask the difficult questions about how to produce a result without the extraordinary ones.

You will be forced to find a system that leverages your ordinary people to the point where they can produce extraordinary results over and over again.

You will be forced to invent innovative system solutions to the people problems that have plagued small businesses (and big businesses as well!) since the beginning of time.

You will be forced to build a business that works.

You will be forced to do the work of Business Development not as a replacement for people development but as its necessary correlate.

3. The Model Will Stand Out as a Place of Impeccable Order

At the core of Rule #3 is the irrepressible fact that in a world of chaos, most people crave order. And it doesn't take a genius to see that the world today is in a state of massive chaos. Wars, famine, crime, violence, inflation, recession, a shifting of traditional forms of social interaction, the threat of nuclear proliferation, HIV, holocaust in all its horrific forms are all communicated instantly and continuously to the fixated consumer, to all of us watching TV.

As Alvin Toffler wrote in his revolutionary book, *The Third Wave,* " . . . most people surveying the world around them today see only chaos. They suffer a sense of personal powerlessness and pointlessness." He went on to say that, "Individuals need life structure. A life lacking in comprehensive structure is an aimless wreck. The absence of structure breeds breakdown. Structure provides the relatively fixed points of reference we need."[1]

It is these "relatively fixed points of reference" that an orderly business provides its customer and its employees in an otherwise disorderly world.

A business that looks orderly says to your customer that your people know what they're doing.

A business that looks orderly says to your people that you know what you're doing.

A business that looks orderly says that while the world may not work, some things can.

A business that looks orderly says to your customer that he can trust in the result delivered and assures your people that they can trust in their future with you.

A business that looks orderly says that the structure is in place.

---

[1] Alvin Toffler, *The Third Wave* (New York: William Morrow and Company, Inc., 1980), pp. 390, 389.

4. All Work in the Model Will Be Documented in Operations Manuals

Documentation says, "This is how we do it here."

Without documentation, all routinized work turns into exceptions.

Documentation provides your people with the structure they need and with a written account of how to "get the job done" in the most efficient and effective way. It communicates to the new employees, as well as to the old, that there is a logic to the world in which they have chosen to work, that there is a technology by which results are produced. Documentation is an affirmation of order.

Again from Toffler: ". . . for many people, a job is crucial psychologically, over and above the paycheck. By making clear demands on their time and energy, it provides an element of structure around which the rest of their lives can be organized."[2]

The operative word here is *clear.*

Documentation provides the clarity structure needs if it is to be meaningful to your people.

Through documentation, structure is reduced to specific means rather than generalized ends, to a literal and simplified task The Technician in each of us needs to understand to do the job at hand.

The Operations Manual—the repository of the documentation—is therefore best described as a company's How-to-Do-It Guide.

It designates the purpose of the work, specifies the steps needed to be taken while doing that work, and

---

[2]Alvin Toffler, *The Third Wave*, p. 389.

summarizes the standards associated with both the process and the result.

Your Prototype would not be a model without one.

5. The Model Will Provide a Uniformly Predictable Service to the Customer

While the business must look orderly, it is not sufficient; the business must also act orderly. It must do things in a predictable, uniform way.

An experience I had not too long ago illustrates the point.

I went to a barber who, in our first meeting, gave me one of the best haircuts I had ever had. He was a master with the scissors and used them exclusively, never resorting to electric shears as so many others do. Before cutting my hair, he insisted on washing it, explaining that the washing made cutting easier. During the haircut, one of his assistants kept my cup of coffee fresh. In all, the experience was delightful, so I made an appointment to return.

When I returned, however, everything had changed. Instead of using the scissors exclusively, he used the shears about 50 percent of the time. He not only didn't wash my hair but never even mentioned it. The assistant did bring me a cup of coffee, but only once, never to return. Nonetheless, the haircut was again excellent.

Several weeks later, I returned for a third appointment. This time, the barber did wash my hair, but after cutting it, preliminary to a final trim. This time he again used the scissors exclusively, but, unlike the first two times, no coffee was served, although he did ask if I would like a glass of wine. At first I thought it might be the assistant's day off, but she soon appeared, busily working with the inventory near the front of the shop.

As I left, something in me decided not to go back. It certainly wasn't the haircut—he did an excellent job. It wasn't the barber. He was pleasant, affable, seemed to know his business. It was something more essential than that.

There was absolutely no consistency to the experience.

The expectations created at the first meeting were violated at each subsequent visit. I wasn't sure what to expect. And something in me wanted to be sure. I wanted an experience *I* could repeat by making the choice to return.

The unpredictability said nothing about the barber, other than that he was constantly—and *arbitrarily*— changing my experience for me. *He* was in control of my experience, not I. And he demonstrated little sensitivity to the impact of his behavior on me. He was running the business for *him*, not for me. And by doing so, he was depriving me of the experience of making a decision to patronize his business for my own reasons, whatever they might have been.

It didn't matter what I wanted.

It didn't matter that I enjoyed the sound of the scissors and somehow equated them with a professional haircut.

It didn't matter that I enjoyed being waited on by his assistant.

It didn't matter that I enjoyed the experience of having my hair washed before he set to work and that I actually believed it would improve the quality of the haircut.

I would have been embarrassed to ask for these things, let alone to give my reasons for wanting them.

They were all so totally emotional, so illogical. How could I have explained them, or justified them, without appearing to be a boob?

What the barber did was to give me a delightful experience and *then take it away.*

It reminded me of my first psychology course in college. I recall the professor talking about the "Burnt Child" Syndrome. This is where a child is alternately punished and rewarded for the same kind of behavior. This form of behavior in a parent can be disastrous to the child; he never knows what to expect or how to act. It can also be disastrous to the customer.

The "Burnt Child," of course, has no choice but to stay with the parent. But the "Burnt Customer" can go someplace else. And he will.

What you do in your model is not nearly as important as doing what you do the same way, each and every time.

6. The Model Will Utilize a Uniform Color, Dress, and Facilities Code

Marketing studies tell us that all consumers are moved to act by the colors and shapes they find in the marketplace.

Different consumer groups simply respond differently to specific colors and shapes.

Believe it or not, the colors and shapes of your model can make or break your business!

Louis Cheskin, founder of the Color Research Institute, wrote about the power of colors and shapes in his book, *Why People Buy.*

Little things that are meaningless from a practical point of view may have great emotional meaning through their symbolism. Images and colors are often great motivating forces.

Some time ago we conducted a study of women shopping in an apparel shop. A young woman wanted to buy a blouse that was available in several colors. She held the blue blouse up to her face and looked into the mirror. She was a blonde and she knew she looked good in blue. She fingered the red one lovingly. She loved the color, she thought, but she said it was too strong and loud. The salesgirl reminded her that yellow was the fashionable color. She could not make up her mind between the color that she looked best in, the color she liked best, and the color in current fashion, so she settled on a gray blouse. It was reported to me a couple of weeks later that she didn't like the gray blouse. "It was dead," she said. She wore it only twice.

Some of the other purchasers of blouses permitted one of the inner drives to win. Some bought blouses because the color flattered them; others chose the color that was in fashion and some took the color they liked. Each chose a color that satisfied the strongest urge or fulfilled the greatest wish. Just think! All this deep psychology in the mere process of buying a blouse.[3]

Your business is the same as the blouse in Cheskin's story. There are colors that work and colors that don't. The colors you show your customer must be scientifically determined and then used throughout your model— on the walls, the floors, the ceiling, the vehicles, the invoices, your people's clothes, the displays, the signs.

The model must be thought of as a package for your one and only product—your business.

[3]Louis Cheskin, *Why People Buy* (New York: Liveright Publishing Corporation, 1959), p. 119.

Just as with colors, there are shapes that work and shapes that don't, on your business card, your signs, your logo, your merchandise displays.

In one test, Cheskin showed that a triangle produced far fewer sales than a circle, and a crest outproduced both by a significant margin!

Imagine, sales increased or lost by the choice of a seemingly meaningless shape!

The shape of your sign, your logo, the type style used on your business cards will have a significant impact on sales whether you care to think about it or not!

Your Prototype must be packaged as carefully as any box of cereal.

Before we go on, let's summarize what we've covered so far.

Go to work *on* your business rather than *in* it.

Go to work on your business as if it were the pre-production prototype of a mass-produceable product.

Think of your business as something apart from yourself, as a world of its own, as a product of your efforts, as a machine designed to fulfill a very specific need, as a mechanism for giving you more life, as a system of interconnecting parts, as a package of cereal, as a can of beans, as something created to satisfy your consumers' deeply held perceived needs, as a place that acts distinctly different from all other places, as a solution to somebody else's problem.

Think of your business as anything but a job!

Go to work *on* your business rather than *in* it, and ask yourself the following questions:

- How can I get my business to work, but without me?

- How can I get my people to work, but without my constant interference?
- How can I systematize my business in such a way that it could be replicated 5,000 times, so the 5,000th unit would run as smoothly as the first?
- How can I own my business, and still be free of it?
- How can I spend my time doing the work I love to do rather than the work I have to do?

If you ask yourself these questions, you'll eventually come face-to-face with the real problem: *that you don't know the answers!*

And that's been the problem all along!

But now it should be different. Because now you know that you don't know. Now you are ready to look the problem squarely in the face.

The problem isn't your business; it never has been.

The problem is you!

It has always been you and will always be you. Until you change, that is.

Until you change your perspective about what a business is and how one works.

Until you begin to think about your business in a totally new way.

Until you accept the undeniable fact that business, even a very small business like yours, is both an art and a science.

And, like art and science, to successfully develop a serious business you need specific information.

Most importantly, to successfully develop a serious business you need a process, a practice, by which to obtain that information and, once obtained, a method with which to put that information to use in your business productively.

What follows is just such a method.

A programmed approach to learning what needs to be learned about your business in order to climb the proverbial ladder.

A proven way to the top that has been successfully implemented by thousands of small businesses just like yours.

We call it the E-Myth Mastery Program.

And it's a process that can change your life!

Sarah looked at me thoughtfully for a moment, and then said, "Let me describe in my own words what I heard you just say." She folded her hands tightly together before her on the table, and, as if for emphasis, leaned toward me.

"What you're saying is that I'm too identified with my business. That I need to separate myself from it: first in the way I think about it, second in the way I feel about it, and third in the way I work in it.

"And what I hear you saying is that it is this identification with my business, my Technician's need to see the business as nothing more or less than me, that is causing me all the pain I'm feeling, all the frustration I experience going to work every day. My belief that, if I'm good, the business will be. That if I work hard enough, the business will succeed. That if I am in touch with everything that goes on in the business, nothing can possibly go wrong.

"And what I hear you saying is that in order for me to be free of my frustration, in order to exercise true control over my business, I need to disidentify with my business. I need to conceive of my business in a radically differently way than I'm accustomed to. I need to conceive of my business as a product. Just like my pies are a product, I need to think of my business like that. And if I were to think that way, I would suddenly have to ask the question: How must my business-as-a-product work in order for it to successfully attract not only customers but also employees who want to work there?

"And the minute I ask that question, I'm already doing business in a totally new way!"

Sarah paused for a moment, as if to let that last thought truly sink in.

"You know," she said quietly, "I can truly say that until this very moment, I had never thought about my business as an idea before. I simply thought of it as a job. A place to go to work. I never even considered there was another way to think about it. But *now!* Now it's getting exciting. An entirely new opportunity. Thinking like this reminds me of my first literature class in high school. My teacher was Mr. Roethke and he had an incredible ability to bring the subject of literature alive. By the time I read the first assignment—it was *Huckleberry Finn*—I couldn't put the book down. These were real people in the book, living out their lives, in real places, overcoming obstacles, terror, love, feelings. *Huckleberry Finn* came alive to me in that first class like no book had before it.

That's what this feels like to me, like we're opening the covers of a new book, not knowing what's inside, but knowing, given the wonderful, rich anticipation that accompanies every new adventure, that nothing will ever be the same again. That's how this all feels to me. That my business will never be the same from this moment on. And neither will I!"

She pressed her hands together, and then leaned back against her chair as if to catch a breath.

"And, if I understand you correctly, that's what you're calling the Franchise Prototype. The Franchise Prototype is the name for my business-as-a-product. It's a way of thinking about my business as one complete thing, a whole, you might say, that looks, acts, and feels in a clearly definable way, apart from me. Independent of me. That if I did all this correctly, All About Pies could be designed, engineered, and manufactured just like any product is: to operate predictably in such a way that causes everyone to want to buy from it, and because it is so predictably responsive to their needs, they would keep on coming back for more. And it's my job to design, engineer, and manufacture All About Pies until it works perfectly without me having to be there all the time.

"And, while I must admit, I'm overwhelmed by the idea of it, it's the most challenging and exciting thought I've had in years!

"And the great thing is, I've already got the business. All I have to do now is to learn how!"

"Sarah," I said, "I couldn't have said it any better. So, let's go on to the next step, the Business Development Process. Because what you have to learn is going to be easier than you think."

For more information, visit us at www.e-myth.com

PART III

Building a Small Business That Works!

10

THE BUSINESS DEVELOPMENT
PROCESS

> Tolerance for failure is a very specific part of the excellent company culture—and that lesson comes directly from the top. Champions have to make lots of tries and consequently suffer some failures or the organization won't learn.
>
> *Thomas J. Peters and Robert H. Waterman Jr.*
> *In Search of Excellence*

Building the Prototype of your business is a continuous process, a Business Development Process. Its foundation is three distinct yet thoroughly integrated activities through which your business can pursue its natural evolution. They are Innovation, Quantification, and Orchestration.

Innovation

Innovation is often thought of as creativity. But as Harvard Professor Theodore Levitt points out, the difference between creativity and Innovation is the difference between thinking about getting things done in the world and getting things done. Says Professor Levitt, "Creativity thinks up new things. Innovation does new things."[1]

The Franchise Revolution has brought with it an application of Innovation that has been almost universally ignored by American business. By recognizing that it is not the *commodity* that demands Innovation but the process by which it is sold, the franchisor aims his innovative energies at the way in which his business does business.

To the franchisor, the entire process by which the business does business is a marketing tool, a mechanism for finding and keeping customers. Each and every component of the business system is a means through which the franchisor can differentiate his business from all other businesses in the mind of his consumer.

Where the *business* is the product, how the business interacts with the consumer is more important than what it sells.

And the how doesn't have to be expensive to be effective. In fact, some of the most powerful Innovations have required little more than the change of a few words, a gesture, the color of clothing.

For example, what does the salesperson in a retail store invariably say to the incoming customer? He says, "May I help you?" Have you ever heard that one before?

And how does the customer invariably respond? He says, "No thanks, just looking." Have you ever said that one before?

---

[1]Theodore Levitt, *Marketing for Business Growth* (New York: McGraw-Hill, 1974), p. 71.

Of course you have!

In fact, it's a universal phenomenon.

Now why do you suppose the salesperson asks that question when he knows that the customer will respond the way he does?

Because the customer responds the way he does, that's why!

If the customer is just looking, the salesperson doesn't have to go to work!

Can you imagine what those few words are costing retailers in this country in lost sales? Here's a perfect opportunity to try a simple and inexpensive Innovation.

THE INNOVATION Instead of asking, "Hi, may I help you?" try "Hi, have you been in here before?" The customer will respond with either a "yes" or a "no." In either case, you are then free to pursue the conversation.

If the answer is yes, you can say, "Great. We've created a special new program for people who have shopped here before. Let me take just a minute to tell you about it."

If the answer is no, you can say, "Great, we've created a special new program for people who haven't shopped here before. Let me take just a minute to tell you about it."

Of course, you'll have to have created a special new program to talk about in either case. But that's the easy part.

Just think. A few simple words. Nothing fancy. But the result is guaranteed to put money in your pocket. How much? That depends on how enthusiastically you do it. The experience of our retail clients tells us that by doing this one thing alone, sales will increase between 10 and 16 percent almost immediately!

Can you believe it? A few simple words and sales instantly go up. Not by just a little bit, mind you, but by a considerable amount! What would you do for a 10- to 16-percent increase in sales?

THE INNOVATION   Again, for salespeople, a six-week test. For the first three weeks, wear a brown suit to work, a starched tan shirt, a brown tie (for men), and well-polished brown shoes. Make certain that all the elements of your suit are clean and well-pressed. For the following three weeks wear a navy blue suit, a good, starched white shirt, a tie with red in it (a pin or a scarf with red in it for women), and highly polished black shoes.

The result will be dramatic: sales will go up during the second three-week period! Why? Because, as our clients have consistently discovered, blue suits outsell brown suits! *And it doesn't matter who's in them.*

Is it any wonder that McDonald's, Federal Express, Disney, Mrs. Field's Cookies, and many more extraordinary companies spend so much time and money on determining how they look? It pays! And it pays consistently, over and over and over again.

THE INNOVATION   The next time you want somebody to do something for you, touch him softly on the arm as you ask him to do it. You will be amazed to find that more people will respond positively when you touch them than when you don't.

Again, to apply this to your business, you or your salespeople should make a point of touching each customer on the elbow, arm, or back some time during the sales process. You will find, as our clients have found, that there will be a measurable increase in sales.

Innovation is the heart of every exceptional business. Innovation continually poses the question: What is standing in the way of my customer getting what he wants from my business?

For the Innovation to be meaningful it must always take the customer's point of view. At the same time, Innovation simplifies your business to its critical essentials. It should make things easier for you and your people in the operation of your business; otherwise it's not Innovation but complication.

Innovation, then, is the mechanism through which your business identifies itself in the mind of your customer and establishes its individuality. It is the result of a scientifically generated and quantifiably verified profile of your customer's perceived needs and unconscious expectations.

It is the skill developed within your business and your people that is constantly asking, "What is the best way to do this?" knowing, even as the question is asked, that we will never discover the best way, but by asking we will assuredly discover a way that's better than the one we know now.

In that regard, I think of Innovation as the "Best Way" skill. It produces a high level of energy in every company within which it's nurtured, fed, and stimulated, energy that in turn feeds everyone the company touches—its employees, customers, suppliers, and lenders. In an innovative company everyone grows.

There's no doubt about it: *Innovation is the signature of a bold, imaginative hand.*

Quantification

But on its own, Innovation leads nowhere. To be at all effective, all Innovations need to be quantified. Without Quantification, how would you know whether the Innovation worked?

By Quantification, I'm talking about the numbers related to the impact an Innovation makes.

For example, ask any group of small business owners how many selling opportunities they had the day before (as we have at E-Myth Worldwide day after day) and I promise you 99 percent of them won't know the answer.

The sad fact is that Quantification is not being done in most businesses. And it's costing them a fortune!

For example, how would you know that by changing the words you use to greet an incoming customer you produced a 16-percent increase in sales unless you quantified it by (1) determining how many people came in the door before the Innovation was put into effect; (2) determining how many people bought products and what the dollar value of those products were before you changed the words and what you said to produce those sales; (3) counting the number of people who came in the door after you changed the words; (4) counting the number of people who purchased something; (5) determining the average unit value of a sale; and (6) determining what the improvement was as a result of your Innovation? These numbers enable you to determine the precise value of your Innovation.

How would you know that wearing a blue suit had a specific monetary impact on your business unless you quantified that impact and had a specific control against which to measure it? The answer is obvious; you wouldn't.

And as I've said, few small business owners do quantify these things, even those who believe in Quantification.

Because few small business owners believe that such apparently insignificant Innovations are really that important!

But ask yourself, if you could increase sales 10 percent by doing something as simple as wearing a blue suit, would you do it? Would you make it important? The answer is as obvious as the question is ridiculous. Of course you would!

And it is the obvious that must be addressed by Quantification at the outset of the Business Development Process.

Begin by quantifying everything related to how you do business.

I mean everything.

How many customers do you see in person each day?

How many in the morning?

In the afternoon?

How many people call your business each day?

How many call to ask for a price?

How many want to purchase something?

How many of product X are sold each day?

At what time of the day are they sold?

How many are sold each week?

Which days are busiest? How busy?

And so forth.

You can't ask too many questions about the numbers.

Eventually, you and your people will think of your entire business in terms of the numbers.

You'll quantify everything.

You'll be able to read your business's health chart by the flow of the numbers.

You'll know which numbers are critical and which are not.

You'll become as familiar with your business's numbers as your doctor is with your blood pressure and pulse rates.

Because without the numbers you can't possibly know where you are, let alone where you're going. With the numbers, your business will take on a totally new meaning.

It will come alive with possibilities.

Orchestration

Once you innovate a process and quantify its impact on your business, once you find something that works better than what preceded it, once you discover how to increase the "yeses" from your customers, your employees, your suppliers, and your lenders—at that point, it's time to orchestrate the whole thing.

Orchestration is the elimination of discretion, or choice, at the operating level of your business.

Without Orchestration, nothing could be planned, and nothing anticipated—by you or your customer. If you're doing everything differently each time you do it, if everyone in your company is doing it by their own discretion, their own choice, rather than creating order, you're creating chaos.

As Theodore Levitt says in his stunning book, *Mar-*

keting for Business Growth, "Discretion is the enemy of order, standardization, and quality."[2]

"If a blue suit works, wear it every single time you're in front of a customer," is the dictum of the disciples of Orchestration.

"If 'Hi, have you been in here before?' works better than anything else you've tried, say it every single time you greet a customer," is the rule of the day from the disciples of Orchestration.

By every disciple of Orchestration I'm referring to anyone who has ever seriously decided to produce a consistent, predictable result in the world of business, no matter what business they are in.

Whether that be Fred Smith at Federal Express, Tom Watson at IBM, Ray Kroc at McDonald's, Walt Disney at Disney, Debbie and Randy Fields at Mrs. Fields' Cookies, or whomever, throughout the course of time.

Because every founder of every great Business Format Franchise company, whether it is franchised or not, knows one thing to be true: *if you haven't orchestrated it, you don't own it!*

And if you don't own it, you can't depend on it.

And if you can't depend on it, you haven't got a franchise.

And without a franchise no business can hope to succeed.

If, by a franchise, you understand that I'm talking about a proprietary way of doing business that differentiates your business from everyone else's.

In short, the definition of a franchise is simply *your unique way of doing business.*

---

[2]Theodore Levitt, *Marketing for Business Growth*, p. 56.

And unless your unique way of doing business can be replicated every single time, you don't own it. You have lost it. And once you've lost it, you're out of business!

The need for Orchestration is based on the absolutely quantifiable certainty that people will do only one thing predictably—be unpredictable.

But for your business to be predictable, your people must be.

Then what?

Then the system must provide the vehicle to facilitate predictability.

To do what?

To give your customer what he wants every single time.

Why?

Because unless your customer gets everything he wants every single time, he'll go someplace else to get it!

Orchestration is the glue that holds you fast to your customers' perceptions.

Orchestration is the certainty that is absent from every other human experience. It is the order and the logic behind the human craving for reason.

Orchestration is as simple as doing what you do, saying what you say, looking like you look—being how and who you are—for as long as it works. For as long as it produces the results you want.

And when it doesn't work any longer, change it!

The Business Development Process is not static.

It's not something you do and then are done with.

It's something you do all the time.

In other words, once you've innovated, quantified, and orchestrated something in your business, you must continue to innovate, quantify, and orchestrate it.

The Business Development Process is dynamic, simply because the world, moving as it does, will not tolerate a stationary object.

The world will collide with whatever you've created, and sooner or later destroy it.

The Business Development Process is that which enables you to preempt the world's changes. It hopefully precedes them, anticipates them, and, if not, at least is infinitely flexible in relationship to them.

In short, Innovation, Quantification, and Orchestration are the backbone of every extraordinary business.

They are the essence of your Business Development Process.

"I need you to help me with something," Sarah said, a look of concern on her face. "I need help coming to grips with this whole subject of Orchestration. It sounds so mechanical, so deadening! When I think of it, I picture a shop full of people working dispassionately, each of them doing things in identically the same way, like robots. Certainly you can't be saying that. But I don't know how else to think about it."

She paused with uncertainty, but then, as though deciding she had made her point, grew quiet and waited for my answer.

"Sarah," I began softly, "if the Business Development Process were only about Orchestration, I would agree with you—it would be deadly. Absent a higher purpose, all habits are. Because that's all that Orchestration really is, Sarah: a habit. A way of doing something habitually.

"The problem is you can't understand the value of an

entire process by separating it from its parts, or its parts
from the process. Because once you separate the parts of
a process, once you take a process apart, there is no process. There is no movement whatsoever. There is only
this thing or that. There is no beginning, no middle, no
end. There is no story; there's only an event, frozen in
time. You might say that apart from its process, the part
of a process is dead. So when you think of Orchestration
absent Innovation and Quantification, you're describing
an action stripped of its purpose, its meaning, its vitality.

"No, to fully understand the role any action—or any
piece of work—plays in the business as a whole, you
have to see it as a part of the whole, not as a thing in
itself. Let me show you what I mean.

"Think back to your aunt's kitchen. Think about the
process of baking a pie. Certainly when you remember
the entire process you and your aunt went through, you
remember much more than any single part of it, isn't
that true?"

Sarah smiled warmly, reliving the experience in
her aunt's kitchen. "Yes, of course that's true," she
responded.

"It all melts together into a sensation, you might
say. Into a picture, and smells, and movements, and
things, fused together with my aunt's remarks and her
laughter and her hands doing the things they did on the
cutting board. Exactly the opposite of what I imagine
Orchestration to be," she said firmly. "In fact, that's
what was so special to me about the kitchen. The creativity of it all. The continuous stream of surprises."

"But think about it, Sarah. Is that really true? Wasn't
there a specific way your aunt taught you to cut the

fruit? A specific way to hold it? A specific way to prepare it? Wasn't there a specific way to do everything
your aunt taught you to do? And wasn't the creativity,
the continuous stream of surprises, a result not just of
the specific work you were doing but of your continuous and exhilarating experience of improving as you
learned how to do those very specific tasks better and
better, until you could do them almost as well as your
aunt?

"Wasn't that where the joy came from? That if you
were resigned to doing one thing, one way, forever,
without ever improving, there would be no joy—there
would only be the same deadening routine? And isn't
that what your aunt taught you as she taught you to
bake pies—the mystery that change can bring?

"So, of course, there needs to be Orchestration,
Sarah. There needs to be a way we do something. There
needs to be a set routine. Because without it, there
would be nothing to improve upon. And without
improvement, there would be no reason to be. We
would be machines. Or, as you called them, 'robots.'
There would be the tyranny of routine. There would be
the monotony and the boredom you so eloquently
describe.

"But with the process, with the continuous Innovation and Quantification that precedes the Orchestration
and that follows it, with this continuous investigation
into the way of work, the work itself becomes key to
our own personal transformation. The work itself
becomes something other than a habit; it becomes an
exploration into who we are and how we express ourselves in relationship to something much larger. First,
the position we fill. Then the function it fills. Then the

business within which the function fulfills both itself and the business, without which it wouldn't exist. Then the world within which the business fulfills its purpose as well as the purpose of the people with whom, and for whom, it comes into contact. And so on, and so forth.

"What I've just described is the thrill of apprenticeship, the learning and growing that you experienced in the kitchen under your aunt's tutelage.

"That's one level of experience. But there are more.

"A second kind of experience is when you begin to develop a certain level of mastery of the orchestrated skills your aunt introduced you to, mastery that comes from your practice. That's the mastery of the craftsperson.

"The craftsperson develops a knowingness about the work she does that bears its own fruit, the fruit of being present, or attentive. The craftsperson learns that within the work she does there is a jewel hiding below the surface. That the thrill of the craft is to discover the jewel. And that there is only one way to discover it: to practice the craft mindlessly. To become one with the work. To polish and polish, as though with one's heart. That there is no way to know when the jewel will show itself, but to trust with all one's heart that one day, when it is least expected, the jewel will be there! It will appear.

"And so the craftsperson is one who has reached that stage of her development where she is content with the work, and only the work, knowing that it is only through being there with one's work that the jewel will reveal itself, and that it is the work, and only the work, raised to the level of near perfection that connects the craftsperson with herself, with her own heart. And so she practices, day in and day out, content to do so, without the thrill of the apprentice to keep her going, but knowing deep inside that there is no place to go but here.

"Unlike the apprentice's stage, the craftsperson's stage is long and relatively serene until that day when the jewel does appear, and with it a stunning explosion of light enraptures the craftsperson and brings with it mastery.

"You've seen mastery before, Sarah. You've seen it in your aunt's face, in her eyes, in the way she spoke to you. For the master, there is only one way and that is to teach another. The master is connected to the apprentice as though to her past. As you are to your childhood. The master knows that the process of growing, of change, of transformation, is always moving, never still. It is in the face of the apprentice that the master sees herself anew. It is in the face of the craftsperson that the master renews her pilgrimage and finds the beauty of giving herself up to work. It is in the face of the work that the master discovers anew why she is so enraptured and, in so doing, brings her rapture to the apprentice to start all over again.

"In much the same way, Orchestration builds upon that which preceded it, and becomes the foundation for that which is about to follow, and, in the process, honors the past, the present, and the future.

"To me, Sarah, that is what the Business Development Process is all about; it is a search, within which the very ordinary things we must do from day-to-day are the essential hub of the wheel around which the search moves.

"On a more practical level, what we've experienced in our work with small businesses is that, as the Business Development Process becomes an integral part of the business, it also becomes an integral part of the communication between the participants. It becomes not only a way of thinking and a way of doing but a way of being as well. You might say that, while going to work on the business, people begin to realize that it is a powerful metaphor for going to work on their lives.

"And that, I believe, is the heart of the process: not efficiency, not effectiveness, not more money, not to 'downsize' or 'get lean,' but to simply and finally create more life for everyone who comes into contact with the business, but most of all, for you, the person who owns it.

"So, I obviously feel passionately about the subject. What you call it doesn't really matter; call it the Business Development Process, Reengineering, TQM, Excellence, or Kaizen—the entire subject becomes a desultory process if it doesn't address the hearts and minds and souls of people.

"*Quality* is just a word, and an empty word at that, if it doesn't include harmony, balance, passion, intention, attention.

"Continuous improvement for its own sake is a waste of time.

"Life is what a business is about, and life is what this work is about. Coming to grips with oneself, in the face of an incredibly complex world that can teach us if we're open to learn.

"In this way, the Business Development Process can be thought of as a metaphor for personal transformation, for coming to grips with real life.

"For developing real skills within a structure of your own design.

"For understanding the dynamics of change, of value, of communication, of thought.

"It's an idea. An idea that we at E-Myth Worldwide have learned to manifest in the practical world. It is a philosophy. It is a cosmology. It is whatever you wish it to be.

"But what it is, in the end, is an opportunity to fulfill whatever is fulfillable in the place you find yourself now, and in any future place you could occupy with enough imagination and enough of a wish."

I suddenly became aware that I had been going on without checking in with Sarah. I've been known to do that at times.

"I'm sorry, Sarah. I got carried away with the *idea* and the sound of my own voice. Do you have any questions? Can I be more specific?"

Sarah touched my hands on the table, and said, "My head is full of questions, but somehow I think you're going to answer them. I just want to thank you for doing what you just did. If you don't mind, could we go on and talk about how all this works?"

I took a sip of tea, and went on.

11

YOUR BUSINESS DEVELOPMENT PROGRAM

And I say to ye all, good friends, that as ye grow in golf, ye
come to see the things ye learn there in every other place.
The grace that comes from such a discipline, the extra feel
in the hands, the extra strength and knowin', all those special powers ye've felt from time to time, begin to enter our
lives.

Michael Murphy
Golf in the Kingdom

Now you understand the task ahead: to think of
your business as though it were the prototype for
5,000 more just like it.

To imagine that someone will walk through your
door with the intention of buying your business—but
only if it works.

And only if it works without a lot of work and without you to work it.

Imagine yourself at that moment. Imagine your
smile inside as you say, "Let me show you how it
works," knowing that not only will it work but it will
work better than any business he's ever seen.

Imagine yourself taking the potential buyer through

your business, explaining each component and how it works with every other component.

How you've innovated systems solutions to people problems, how you've quantified the results of those innovations, and how you've orchestrated the innovations so that they produce the same results every single time.

Imagine yourself introducing the potential buyer of your business to your people, and standing by while they proudly explain their accountabilities to the fascinated stranger.

Imagine how impressed the potential buyer of your business would be upon being presented with such order, such predictability, such irreproachable control.

Imagine the results of your Business Development Program.

Your Business Development Program is the step-by-step process through which you convert your existing business—or the one you're about to create—into a perfectly organized model for thousands more just like it.

Your Business Development Program is the vehicle through which you can create your Franchise Prototype.

The Program is composed of seven distinct steps:

1. Your Primary Aim
2. Your Strategic Objective
3. Your Organizational Strategy
4. Your Management Strategy
5. Your People Strategy
6. Your Marketing Strategy
7. Your Systems Strategy

Let's get started.

12

YOUR PRIMARY AIM

The chief characteristic of the volitional act is the existence of a purpose to be achieved; the clear vision of an aim.

Robert Assagioli
The Act of Will

I doubt that by now you'd be surprised to find out that I don't believe your business to be the first order of business on our agenda.

You are.

Nor will you be surprised to hear that I don't believe your business is your life, though it does and can play a significantly important role in your life.

But before you can determine what that role will be, you must ask yourself these questions: What do I value most? What kind of life do I want? What do I want my life to look like, to feel like? Who do I wish to be?

Your Primary Aim is the answer to all these questions.

Consider it from another perspective.

I'd like you to imagine that you are about to attend one of the most important occasions of your life.

It will be held in a room sufficiently large to seat all

of your friends, your family, your business associates—anyone and everyone to whom you are important and who is important to you.

Can you see it?

The walls are draped with deep golden tapestries. The lighting is subdued, soft, casting a warm glow on the faces of your expectant guests. Their chairs are handsomely upholstered in a golden fabric that matches the tapestries. The golden carpeting is deeply piled.

At the front of the room is a dais, and on the dais a large, beautifully decorated table, with candles burning at either end.

On the table, in the center, is the object of everyone's attention. A large, shining, ornate box. And in the box is . . . you! Stiff as the proverbial board.

Do you see yourself lying in the box, not a dry eye in the room?

Now, listen.

From the four corners of the room comes a tape recording of your voice. Can you hear it? You're addressing your guests. You're telling them the story of your life.

How would you like that story to go?

That's your Primary Aim.

What would you like to be able to say about your life after it's too late to do anything about it?

That's your Primary Aim.

If you were to write a script for the tape to be played for the mourners at your funeral, how would you like it to read?

That's your Primary Aim.

And once you've created the script, all you need to do is make it come true.

All you need to do is begin living your life as if it were important.

All you need to do is take your life seriously.

To create it intentionally.

To actively make your life into the life you wish it to be.

Simple? Yes.

Easy? No.

But absolutely essential if your business is to have any meaning beyond work.

Because if your business is going to become an integral part of that tape, if your business is going to make a major contribution to the realization of your dream, if your business is going to become a significant component of your Primary Aim, you have to let your business know what that Aim is!

And how can you expect to do that, if you don't know what it is?

Do you see why your Primary Aim is so important to the success of your business?

With no clear picture of how you wish your life to be, how on earth can you begin to live it?

How would you know what first step to take?

How would you measure your progress?

How would you know where you were?

How would you know how far you had gone?

How would you know how much farther you had yet to go?

Without your Primary Aim, you wouldn't. Indeed, you couldn't. It would be virtually impossible.

As with Mature companies, I believe great people to be those who know how they got where they are, and what they need to do to get where they're going.

Great people have a vision of their lives that they practice emulating each and every day.

They go to work on their lives, not just in their lives.

Their lives are spent living out the vision they have of their future, in the present. They compare what they've done with what they intended to do. And where there's a disparity between the two, they don't wait very long to make up the difference.

They go to work on their lives, not just in their lives.

I believe it's true that the difference between great people and everyone else is that great people create their lives actively, while everyone else is created by their lives, passively waiting to see where life takes them next.

The difference between the two is the difference between living fully and just existing.

The difference between the two is living intentionally and living by accident.

Let me repeat once more that great quote by Don Juan in Carlos Castaneda's *A Separate Peace:* "The difference between a warrior and an ordinary man is that a warrior sees everything as a challenge, while an ordinary man sees everything as either a blessing or a curse."

So before you start your business, or before you return to it tomorrow, ask yourself the following questions:

- What do I wish my life to look like?
- How do I wish my life to be on a day-to-day basis?
- What would I like to be able to say I truly know in my life, about my life?
- How would I like to be with other people in my life—my family, my friends, my business associ-

ates, my customers, my employees, my community?
- How would I like people to think about me?
- What would I like to be doing two years from
now? Ten years from now? Twenty years from
now? When my life comes to a close?
- What specifically would I like to learn during my
life—spiritually, physically, financially, techni-
cally, intellectually? About relationships?
- How much money will I need to do the things I
wish to do? By when will I need it?

These are just a few of the questions you might ask
yourself in the creation of your Primary Aim.

The answers become the standards against which
you can begin to measure your life's progress. In the
absence of such standards, your life will drift aimlessly,
without purpose, without meaning.

In that regard, your Primary Aim is the vision necessary to bring your business to life and your life to your
business.

It provides you with a purpose.

It provides you with energy.

It provides you with the grist for your day-to-day
mill.

"That's what's been missing in my business," Sarah all
but shouted. "Me! How could I have been so oblivious
to something so obvious?"

"Don't be so hard on yourself," I said. "We are all
oblivious. Join the club. Let me tell you a story.

"There was once a young man who had recently
turned forty whose life seemed to be going nowhere.
Somehow he had never grabbed hold of a career. His life

had no purpose. College had somehow eluded him. In his first year at UCLA, he couldn't find anything to hold his attention and he quit. He studied music—many said brilliantly—as a boy, but in his early adult years failed to find the conviction he needed to pursue it.

"Many different things attracted him—music, religion, mysticism, writing poetry, drugs, writing pulp fiction, money—none of them permanently. He took whatever jobs came along, and, because of his natural and varied talents, he did whatever he did well, but even then none of the jobs turned into anything with a future, at least not a future that attracted him. After leaving college at midterm, he drove to New York City to study art, quickly changed his mind, and joined the Army, which sent him to Korea. His father died suddenly, bringing him home to care for his mother and two younger siblings.

"Some time after, he met an exciting woman, took off to Europe where they traveled from country to country on a motor scooter, and where he played saxophone and drew religious figures on the streets in front of cathedrals to earn enough money to eat. Finally out of money and tired of the game, he and his woman friend were repatriated by the U.S. government and returned to New York City where they contracted to drive a New York City yellow cab to L.A. to deliver it to its new owner.

"When he was twenty-five, they married, had two children, moved to San Francisco, where the young man sold encyclopedias for a living, played saxophone on occasion, and became over time less young. Their life was a running battle. Eventually, after one too many rages about his wife's abuse of alcohol, her infidelity, and his lack of purpose, the whole thing came tumbling down into divorce.

"He immediately met a much younger woman, whose eyes shined like his ex-wife's didn't, who read his poetry and was touched by it, who listened to his music and was awed by it, was satisfied just to sit by his side, no questions asked. And though he continued to sell encyclopedias, and though his heartfelt need for connecting with something that smacked of purpose continued to pain him privately throughout all of this, his life took a more positive turn with this new young woman who eventually became his second wife.

"He went back to college, left the book business, studied contracting and construction so he could work with his hands rather than his mouth, moved with his new, willing wife to southern California, and maneuvered himself into framing jobs from which he was fired time after time until he learned how to pull it off.

"By this time, he was a man in his late thirties beginning to do work that kids twenty years younger than him did. They regarded him on the job as something of a freak. His beard by now was down to his chest, his hair hung down over his shoulders; he wrote poetry at night, played jazz on the weekend, ate burritos with the Mexicans on the job, smoked dope in the evenings, and dreamed crazily about the future when he and his young wife would buy twenty acres in Mendocino County, build their own house with their own hands, raise a family, and have his two girls from his first marriage move in with them when everything was ready.

"They had a tiny one-bedroom house in Santa Ana, California, drove a '52 Chevy pickup, and along with their Great Dane named Dan and a little black poodle named Murray, they lived in a sense-steaming daze that seemed at the time close to what the perfect life must be like.

"But, as with all good things, this too came to an end, when our young man, turning older, pursued by the demons of some indefinable muse, decided to move back north, now that they had their act together, saved up enough from living the right life, hands crusted and gnarly from 'honest' work, body brown and beautiful from putting his muscles on the line, brain filled with the poetry he had written, the music he had renewed, and the dope he had smoked, knowing that it was time to become the contractor he had set out to become three years before, and that all it would take was one sizable kick to get them moving toward what he knew would be the fine resolution of his up-to-now raggedy search.

"He and his wife and his Great Dane, Dan, and his poodle named Murray, plus whatever else they had accumulated in the few years he spent working with his hands rather than his mouth in southern California, piled it all up in the '52 Chevy pickup and moved back to the San Francisco they had come from not that long before.

"It was then that the big shift took place and the unpredictable happened. Our now thirty-eighty-year-old hero and his young wife, along with the dogs and the pickup, were invited to move in temporarily with his sister and her husband while negotiating the purchase of their 'Mendocino Acres.' His brother-in-law had the idea that our hero would do well consulting—in the area in which he was a tested expert, sales—with his advertising agency's hi-tech small business clients, until such time, of course, that our hero settled down with his young bride on their 'Mendocino Acres' to follow his true calling.

"Understand, everyone knew that that was going to

happen. Nobody doubted it. Full of the robust idealism that had marked his youthful passing, he was, without any doubt whatsoever, going to realize his vision; the twenty acres were all but his—it simply required the doing. Of course, there was also the contractor's license and the money, but no one thought that any of that would prove insurmountable.

"After all, here was a man who had lived a life that baffled good reason. Whatever he chose to do, he did. Whatever he did, he was good at. No matter that once he did it, he grew tired of it. He chose to do that, too. To his friends and his family he was, if not unexplainable, certainly someone to be noticed, at times in amazement, and at times with pity; but, never without awe, because who knew what this man was going to do next? And somehow, they all, in their own private way, envied him! Can you believe that? They envied him because he seemed so free! Despite the perpetual trouble he found himself in. Despite his lack of direction. Despite his whimsical and sometimes dangerous philosophy, there was no denying it, this man, although getting older, sometimes precipitously, was living a romantic adventure they write movies about, or, if not that, a pitiful tragedy.

"By anyone's standards, he was living pretty close to the edge. Here's a guy on the cusp of middle age with a long beard, a young wife, two dogs, and a pickup, without a home of their own, living with family, searching for property they couldn't possibly afford, with hardly a thought in his head that anything was wrong at all with this picture, about to step on those moving stairs to somewhere that he was totally unprepared for.

"And take the step he did. And it was a stunner! He was, thanks to his brother-in-law's good intentions, suddenly set adrift in a world that could have been another planet for all he knew. In Silicon Valley. Calling on techies who owned businesses whose names he couldn't even pronounce at first attempt, making stuff he didn't even know existed. He was dumbfounded by the magnitude of his ignorance. And yet, something called him to stay. They asked him, 'How can you help me?' He answered, 'I don't know.' They asked him, 'What do you know about my business?' He answered, 'Nothing.' They looked at him for a long time. He sat and looked back, and just thought. They said to him, 'Why don't you come back after you've had some time to think about it.' He said he would. And he did. Because he knew something was there.

"Understand, here's a guy who had been selling encyclopedias to people at night, in front of their television sets, or on the dining room table. Watching their faces suspiciously regard him as someone who came out of the night, until he spread out the encyclopedia and the vividly colored panels that showed all the books graphically alive: the maps, the transparencies of the human body, the endless list of topics, of wonders the world withheld from them in their ordinary lives, the promise to their children, even their children to come, of education, of knowledge, of information, long before the Information Age had arrived.

"Here their eyes would awaken and lighten up to all these colorful pictures of what was possible, and now, almost within their reach, pending a decision. He had done that late at night, grinding away in front of Frank and Marge until finally Frank, with his last breath, would say sort of covertly,'Well, Marge, whad'ya think? Think we should do it?' And he would sit there, our thirty-something hero, waiting without a movement, without a whisper of encouragement to Marge, let alone to Frank, waiting for the inevitable 'yes' or 'no,' either of which would turn him back out into the night to, if he was lucky, go another round, at Ben and Mary's, with all the little kids hanging on the pictures and making messes on his laminated plates.

"To this guy, this world, this Silicon Valley, was a miracle! 'And I get to do this during the day?!' And so, visit them he would. All the while feeling stupid, knowing nothing about their world, or their business, or the little weird things they made there, the little black boxes with their arcane significance so far beyond his experience of coffee tables and poetry and music and framing and pitching and closing, this intricate little world of theirs that lived in some cubicle inside of their foreign, tight, screwy little brains. And yet, intuitively, he knew that he knew something that they needed. He knew that there was something waiting there for him, something his peculiar life had—in some strange, inexplicable way—prepared him for, something only someone who had lived in such an unconscious, cataclysmic, totally disorganized, yet always passionate state, doing this and that, could fully appreciate.

"And it was then that the curtain lifted. The curtain between the world that was theirs and the world that was his. But most of all, the curtain that stood between himself and himself, the curtain that separated him from his life.

"It was then that he realized with a suddenness that made him giddy that, while he didn't understand their business, neither did they! And in that one shuddering instant of truth our hero was reborn. He discovered an entirely new life.

"And with the discovery of his new life, there came for the very first time in his life the beginning of some purpose: to never let the curtain down again, to never allow the curtain to cover what was hiding there behind it. That the world was nothing like he had believed it to be. That no one knew what he had believed they knew. That everything was just like he had thought it was, a mystery, but that he wasn't the only one who didn't know what was going on. What he learned in Silicon Valley is that no one knew what was going on! It was completely open to interpretation. And his guess was as good as anyone's. My God, probably even better.

"After all, he had met Frank and Marge face-to-face. He had survived the worst of the worst confrontations. He had even been attacked by a German shepherd dog while he was attempting to make his final close. Right across the kitchen table! Who in Silicon Valley could say that? And live to tell about it. Yo, and he had even made the sale! Walked out with a torn contract in hand and a check. Who said little black boxes were dangerous? Who said there was anything to fear, anything he couldn't understand?"

I stopped long enough to feel how much this story had touched Sarah and how much she wanted to ask the obvious question, but I had to finish, so I went on.

"And so that chapter of our hero's life was closed and a new chapter opened. He moved into his early forties and the end of his second marriage, which also, by this time, had produced a child—his third daughter—another love of his life who could not, as no child can ever do, repair a broken marriage. During the years that followed, he became about the best anyone could be in his now chosen profession. He learned the secrets he thought were hidden. He married a woman far bigger than the others, had two more children, fought battles with his ignorance at times titanic in scope, moved through one obstacle after another, wrote books, spoke throughout the world, built a great business, only to watch it almost fail, persisted in building it up again, lanced, jabbed, wrestled, grappled, laughed, sang, loved, and roared, and through it all, remembered one simple thing that meant more to him than anything else he had ever thought: the curtain, the curtain. *Keep the curtain up at all cost.*

"Because it is the curtain that kept him shrouded in darkness. And it's the darkness that holds out the light. It is the light, the openness, the clearing of all the obstacles to knowing that had become his true purpose: to be open. To be awake, to be available to what's really going on, to give up false beliefs.

"And for only one reason: his life was at stake!

"And that's the point, Sarah.

"It's not your business you have to fear losing. It's something much bigger than that. It's your Self.

"And that's what this whole thing is about.

"What truths are your curtain hiding from you? What misunderstanding keeps you where you are, in the past, in the dark, shrouded in your limited beliefs, shrinking from the world, from the light on the other side of the curtain?

"Until you lift the curtain, Sarah, until you dare to pull the mask off the world's face, until you move beyond your Comfort Zone, you will never know what it is you were missing out there.

"It's you, Sarah. It's you that's waiting out there for you to find on the other side of the curtain.

"I know, Sarah, because the man I've been telling you about is me. When the curtain lifted, I learned something.

"That there's no one else out there but you!"

13

YOUR STRATEGIC OBJECTIVE

'Your arrows do not carry,' observed the Master, 'because they do not reach far enough spiritually.'

Eugen Herrigel
Zen and the Art of Archery

Once you have a picture of how you want your life to be, and you come to the realization that it's more than just things to have and things to do, once you realize that what you and I really want is to have the room, the openness, to expand, to grow, to be more of ourselves, whatever that means, and to find out what that means is what's most important to us, once you see that, you can then turn to the business that's going to help you get there; you can then turn to the development of your Strategic Objective.

Your Strategic Objective is a very clear statement of what your business has to ultimately do for you to achieve your Primary Aim.

It is the vision of the finished product that is and will be your business.

In this context, your business is a means rather than an end, a vehicle to enrich your life rather than one that drains the life you have.

Your Strategic Objective is *not* a business plan. It is a product of your Life Plan, as well as your Business Strategy and Plan. Your Life Plan shapes your life, and the business that is to serve it. Your Business Strategy and Plan provide the structure within which your business is intended to operate over time to fulfill your Life Plan. Your Business Strategy and Plan are a way of communicating to anyone you must communicate to the direction your business is going, how it intends to get there, and the specific benchmarks it will need to hit in order for the Strategy and Plan to work.

Your Business Strategy and Plan are also useful for marketing your business to those who are important to you: your banker, your investors, and your strategic alliances in the business community.

But unless your Business Strategy and Plan can be reduced to a set of simple and clearly stated standards, it will do more to confuse you than to help.

Your Strategic Objective is just such a list of standards.

It is a tool for measuring your progress toward a specific end.

It is designed for implementation, not for rationalization.

It is a template for your business, to make certain that the time you invest in it produces exactly what you want from it.

Let's take a closer look at some of the standards that need to be included in your Strategic Objective.

The First Standard: Money

The first standard of your Strategic Objective is money. Gross revenues. How big is your vision? How big will your company be when it's finally done? Will it be a $300,000 company? A million-dollar company? A $500-million company?

If you don't know the answer, how can you possibly know whether your business can help you realize your Primary Aim?

But gross revenues alone are not enough. You also have to know what your gross profits are going to be, your pretax profits, your after-tax profits.

At this point you come face-to-face with the first dilemma encountered by everyone going into business. How can you possibly know now what your business is going to produce in sales that far in the future?

The answer is, you can't! But it doesn't matter. At the beginning of your business, any standards are better than no standards. Creating money standards is not just strategically necessary for your business; it is strategically necessary for your life, for the realization of your Primary Aim.

Indeed, the first question you must always ask when creating standards for your Strategic Objective is: What will serve my Primary Aim?

The first question about money then becomes: How much money do I need to live the way I wish? Not in income but in assets. In other words, how much money do you need in order to be independent of work, to be free?

In fact, there is ultimately only one reason to create a business of your own, and that is to sell it!

To do it, to finish it, and then to get paid for it!

Just like Ray Kroc did, to create your Franchise Prototype, to turn-key your business, to create a business that really works, and then sell it.

How much do you want for it? Ten times earnings? Twenty times earnings?

When do you want it? Three years from now? Five years?

Why would anyone buy it?

Because it works!

And it works because you built it that way. You built it so that it would work better than anyone else's business. You invented a turn-key solution to your specific kind of business's problems. A little money machine. An absolutely predictable little business that does what it promises to do every single time.

A business that can give you everything you want.

And because it can give you everything you want, it can give your prospective buyer everything he wants.

At this point another set of standards are immediately brought into the picture. Because once you've created a set of financial standards for your life, once you know what it is your business needs to provide you with as a return on your investment, it becomes obvious that the business must have a realistic chance of achieving those standards, of producing that return on your investment.

How can you know whether or not it does?

By determining whether your business is an Opportunity Worth Pursuing.

The Second Standard: An Opportunity Worth Pursuing

An Opportunity Worth Pursuing is a business that can fulfill the financial standards you've created for your Primary Aim and your Strategic Objective.

If it is reasonable to assume that it can, the business is worth pursuing.

If it is unreasonable to assume that it can, then no matter how exciting, interesting, or appealing the business is, forget it. Walk away from it. It will consume too much of your precious time and prevent you from finding a true Opportunity Worth Pursuing.

How do you know whether you have an Opportunity Worth Pursuing? Look around. Ask yourself: Does the business I have in mind alleviate a frustration experienced by a large enough group of consumers to make it worth my while?

This standard fulfills two primary requirements of your Strategic Objective. It tells you what kind of business you're creating while it defines who your customer will be. It tells you what you need to sell and to whom.

What Kind of Business Am I In?

Ask anyone what kind of business they're in and they'll instinctively respond with the name of the commodity they sell. "We're in the computer business." Or, "We're in the hot tub business." Always the commodity, never the product.

What's the difference?

The commodity is the thing your customer actually walks out with in his hand.

The product is what your customer feels as he walks out of your business.

What he feels about your business, not what he feels about the commodity.

Understanding the difference between the two is what creating a great business is all about.

Charles Revson, the founder of Revlon and an extraordinarily successful entrepreneur, once said about his company: "In the factory Revlon manufactures cosmetics, but in the store Revlon sells hope."

The commodity is cosmetics; the product, hope.

In a Chanel television commercial in the 1980s, an incredibly handsome man and a strikingly beautiful woman are alone while music plays hypnotically in the background.

The scene shifts quickly and frequently to other shots, such as a tall, erect building.

So far there hasn't been a sound except for the music that supports this suggestive visual ballet.

The black shadow of an airplane moves vertically up the building.

She approaches him.

The music continues.

He says, "Can I ask you a question?" in a voice filled with intimacy and invitation.

We don't hear her answer.

We just see her tilt her head back, close her eyes, and open her mouth slightly.

Suddenly, the message: "Share the Fantasy. Chanel."

Not a word about perfume. That's the commodity. The commercial is selling the product—fantasy.

The commercial is saying, "Buy Chanel and this fantasy can be yours."

What's your product? What feeling will your customer walk away with? Peace of mind? Order? Power? Love? What is he really buying when he buys from you?

The truth is, nobody's interested in the commodity.

People buy feelings.

And as the world becomes more and more complex, and the commodities more varied, the feelings we want become more urgent, less rational, more unconscious.

How your business anticipates those feelings and satisfies them is your product.

And the demographics and psychographics associated with your customer will predetermine how you do that.

Who Is My Customer?

Every business has a Central Demographic Model. That is, a most probable customer. And that customer has a whole set of characteristics through which you can define him—age, sex, income, family status, education, profession, and so forth.

Demographics is the science of marketplace reality. It tells you who your customer is.

Your Central Demographic Model customer buys for very particular reasons, none of which are rational or even explicable! Yet he buys, or doesn't.

The motivations that propel him in either direction constitute your Central Psychographic Model.

Psychographics is the science of perceived marketplace reality. It tells you why your customer buys.

So when you ask, "Is this business an Opportunity Worth Pursuing?" the only way to tell is to determine how many selling opportunities you have (your customers' demographics) and how successfully you can satisfy the emotional or perceived needs lurking there (your customers' psychographics).

Standards Three Through?

There is no specific number of standards in your Strategic Objective. There are only specific questions that need to be answered.

- When is your Prototype going to be completed? In two years? Three? Ten?
- Where are you going to be in business? Locally? Regionally? Nationally? Internationally?
- How are you going to be in business? Retail? Wholesale? A combination of the two?
- What standards are you going to insist upon regarding reporting, cleanliness, clothing, management, hiring, firing, training, and so forth?

You can begin to see that the standards you create for your business will shape both your business and the experience you have of your business.

In fact, the standards of your Strategic Objective create the tension that draws the future model of your business and the way it actually appears today closer to one another.

As we saw earlier, standards create the energy by which the best companies, and the most effective people, produce results.

It was eleven o'clock Monday morning, one week following my last meeting with Sarah. It was the one day of the week All About Pies was closed.

We decided to spend the day together to talk about her business.

As she walked up to the table in the restaurant where we had decided to meet, I could see her excitement. She was a much different Sarah than when I had seen her a week earlier. Her eyes were clear, her body exuberant. She looked much younger. She also looked like she had a lot to talk about.

The restaurant was owned by a friend of mine. We had done a lot of work together in his start-up years and so it was a place where I could take a table and spend as much time as I needed without being rushed out the door. In fact, it was a wonderful place to provide a new client with some clarity about what a business could do when done well.

Sarah sat down and immediately began to talk.

I poured her some coffee.

"It seems for the first time in my life, I truly have come to some understanding about what I want. It is important for me to tell you how much I appreciate what you've given me. But, having said that, I realized, from almost the moment you left last week, that I would never allow myself again to be consumed by the work of my business. It became obvious to me, with a clarity that's almost impossible to describe, how big a price I have been paying for being so obsessed with my work. And, once I realized it, I swear, it was like I was suddenly and forever free of it. Something truly freeing happened to me that night.

"And it's not as though I haven't been working for the past six days. I have. Business has to go on, after all. But this past week was not the way it was before. While one part of me was doing the work—I guess that's the part you would call The Technician—part of me stayed removed from it. Part of me wasn't taken at all by the work I was doing. And, remember how I told you that I didn't think I was entrepreneurial? Well, I suddenly realized that I am! That I've always had an entrepreneurial part in me. That what you call The Entrepreneur, I have always thought of as my spirit.

" 'My spirit' is what my aunt called it. She used to say to me, 'Sarah, feed your spirit. It is your spirit which gives you life.' I remember as a little girl, it was my spirit that always got me into trouble. It was my spirit that my teachers complained about so much. They used to say to my parents, 'If it weren't for Sarah's spirit, she would be doing much better in school than she does.' It was my spirit that would dream when I was in the classroom, rather than pay attention to what was going on around me.

"I used to fantasize about things all the time—my head went to the strangest places. Anything could set me off. And while that part of me would really seem to tick my teachers and my parents off, my aunt always seemed to nurture it. 'You need to be very gentle with your spirit, Sarah,' she used to say to me. 'It needs to be free, but it also needs you to direct its attention. Too much of one, and not enough of the other, and your spirit will take off like a wild horse. That's how you need to think of your spirit, Sarah, like a wild horse. Part of it is there to serve you, and another part to serve itself. The thing you need to learn is which part is which. If you put it behind a fence, you will kill it. But if you leave it to come and go as it pleases, you will never understand it.'

"And I see that's what I've been doing these past three years," Sarah said to me. "I've put a fence around my spirit, around my entrepreneurial nature, without even realizing it. But what I really came to understand this past week is that I've been doing that, putting a fence around my spirit, for a long, long time. My parents taught me how to do it; my teachers taught me how to do it. And, like a good little girl, I learned the lesson well. But now the wild horse is free! Now I'm back in the kitchen with my aunt again. Now I really understand what my aunt was doing with me in the kitchen all those years ago. She wasn't teaching me how to bake pies; she was baking me! She was teaching me about the wild horse, about my spirit. About creativity.

"And when you talked about The Entrepreneur, it all came back to me with a rush. My aunt, the kitchen, the pies, the dreaming in the classroom, the secret places I used to go hide when I was a little girl. And how I stopped hiding in those places a long time ago, and how much I miss it!

"What I've come to realize is that I've confused baking good pies with what my aunt was really talking to me about. I thought that baking good pies was it, when it wasn't. It never has been. And it never will be again.

"So, back to my business," she continued. "It's clear to me now that what I wish to do is to develop it, grow it, and be free of it to do whatever else it is I wish to do, even though, right now, at this very moment, I couldn't for the life of me tell you what that is."

"Try," I said. "Try to tell me as best you can."

She smiled. "You're just like my aunt; she never let me off the hook either.

"Okay, I'll try. Why not—what else do we have to do?"

She closed her eyes for a moment and seemed to

gather herself. And then she began to speak softly, as though to herself.

"I'm a little girl again. When I still had my hiding places. Before I lost my spirit. It's summer, and I'm lying in bed looking up at the ceiling in my room, feeling the cool summer breeze floating through the open window. There's nothing I have to do; there's no place I have to be. It's the most wonderful feeling of my life, lying here like this, opening my eyes, closing them, dreaming, smelling the wonderful summer smells, the smell of cut grass, the smell of the water sprinkling on the lawn, the fullness of it.

"And then I begin to dream, first in colors, nothing specific, just colors, floating above my head, like crystals and flowers and blossoms of light in glowing colors. And then the colors take form—they are me, and they are also something else. I'm walking by the stream that runs across our land, about 500 feet from the house, down where the four oaks stand. We have these four oaks—huge, gnarled trees that stand like a miniature forest at the corner of our property. My aunt and I called them 'Four Oaks,' as though they were another country. And I used to go there as a little girl and imagine I was in another country.

"I'm in 'Four Oaks' now, in my mind, as I lie there in my bed, as I used to do time after time. And it's there where my wild horse waited for me. He is standing in the center of the 'Four Oaks,' his body glistening in the shade, black as black can be. I walk up to him and touch his face, and he shudders and pulls away from me. For a moment we watch each other without moving, and then, he's gone! He whirls around and speeds off, his mane and tail streaming, out of the trees, through the stream, over the hill on the other side of the stream, and out of sight. I'm suddenly aware of the sweet summer breeze again, as it softly touches my face, and I'm in bed, hugging myself under the covers, thrilled to be alive on such a wonderful summer morning when there's nothing at all I have to do but this."

Tears were streaming down Sarah's cheeks. Tears of something precious lost and then found. There was a radiant smile on her face. The tears also welled up in my eyes, watching her, understanding what this meant to her, and understanding at the same time what this meant to me.

We ate lunch almost without talking and then settled down into an afternoon of conversation. The waiter brought us a pot of tea. Sarah poured herself and me a cup, and then I began.

"Tell me," I said, "now that you have a better feeling for what your business can do for you, why don't you try to describe it to me. Why don't you begin to describe your Strategic Objective?"

"Okay," she began. "I've given some thought to this," she smiled, almost bashfully.

I was thinking to myself, as she finished collecting her thoughts, that I've seen that smile dozens, if not hundreds, of times before when owners of a business begin to imagine their company as something bigger than they ever dared to imagine before, and as they tell it to me or to someone else. It's as though they are embarrassed to be seen imagining something bigger than they are; as though they are overreaching, being presumptuous. I suspect they must have experienced something similar when they were children, telling their parents or their teachers about a fanciful idea they had, and feeling the disappointment and shame that comes from being told that you're being unrealistic, that you're dreaming, hearing them say, "You can't do that." And finding themselves alone as children with their dreams that they dared not share again. How, without even realizing it, our parents and our teachers take our "spirit" away.

But, like I knew she would, Sarah continued without embarrassment now, fully taken by the pictures she was describing. This was her business, this was her idea, and she could see it as clearly as anything.

"I see my business about seven years from now," she said. "There are four locations: the one I have now and three more." She named the three communities adjoining hers.

"The name of the business is the same. There's no need to change that. The business is all about pies, all about the experience of pies my aunt gave to me. It's that experience I wish to give to other people. Not only my customers but the people I hire. I want everyone to know, somehow, that All About Pies is a metaphor for something much finer.

"I see the shops producing annual sales of $450,000 each, for a total of $1,800,000 a year. I'm not totally certain what the net profit will be, but I've decided that it should be about 15 percent, or $67,500 for each shop, for a total of $270,000 for the four. I feel that that's a reasonable profit to shoot for, even though today I'm only producing about 11 percent, after my income, I mean.

"That means if I sell the business in seven years, given a realistic price/earnings ratio, I think it's called, I should be able to sell the business for more than $1 million. One million dollars in seven years—that's my dream," she said to me, smiling, as though she could already see the money in the bank. "Because, first, I won't ever need any more money than that to do everything I have ever wanted, and second, because it's really a great round number to shoot for. It sort of makes everything I need to do really concrete.

"Before I can open my second shop, I realize I've got to get this one operating without me. And so, one of the first things I'm going to do—and I've already begun to do this since we met last week—is to document all of the things I really know how to do today. For example, I know how to bake a great pie. And I know that I can document how I do that, so that's one of the first places I'm going to begin. But I'm getting ahead of myself. Let me tell you what my business will look like when it's done, so you can really get a feel for it.

"My aunt used to say that one of the problems we have in our lives is that we don't express our caring deeply or often enough. She used to say that when we were in the kitchen cutting the apples, or something like that. She'd say, 'When we cut apples, we're doing something important. And God is giving us something important, not only the apple, which is important enough, but the kitchen, and the knife, and the company we're giving each other. So when we cut the apples, we need to remember that, and hold them just right, and slice into them with just the appropriate force, not too much, not too little.' She would say, 'Hold my hand while I cut the apple. Do you feel what I mean? Not too much, and not too little. Too much and you are taken away by the task. Too little and the apple doesn't get cut.'

"Anyway, in my business I want to express 'not too much and not too little.' I want the business to be an expression of 'our caring deeply and often enough.' I want the business, All About Pies, to be all about caring, not about pies.

"And if the business is all about caring, then everything we do in the business, everything the business 'looks, acts, and feels like,' " she said to me with a smile, remembering the story I had shared with her about Tom Watson, "then everything the business is will be a reflection of that, a reflection of caring. Caring will be the true product of my business, not pies.

"So I see All About Pies as a model for everyone who comes into contact with it. And what's so exciting about that is I know I can do it! My aunt taught me how. I know what it means to care enough about the kitchen to scrub it down until it gleams. I know what it means to care enough about the knives to sharpen them until they're razor-keen. I know what it means to select the finest fruit, to spend time smelling it, holding it, looking at it, to know exactly when it's ready. To make absolutely certain of that, my aunt planted her own garden, her own trees. And we would see that only the best of organic fertilizers were used, and so I know that All About Pies needs to grow its own fruit in its own gardens. And that's something I just realized this week!

"So I now feel certain that, in order for All About Pies to become what I can imagine it to become, it won't be enough for my employees to just work in the shop—they need to learn everything just as I did when I was a girl working with my aunt. All About Pies will be to them what my aunt was to me!

"And I know I can do that!" she said to me, again

passionately. "It's as real to me now as my aunt was to me then.

"So each shop will produce pies with fruit from a central organic garden. Which means I'm going to have to find one to buy, or land that I'm going to have to plant, centrally located between the shops so that each has the access it needs.

"What it also means is that the shops are only going to bake pies from fruit that's in season here, when it's in season. That's all my aunt ever did. I'm not going to use fruit from anyplace other than my own gardens, and that is going to be something unique about All About Pies that differentiates it from every other bakery or small pie shop. Truly homegrown. With homegrown gentle care.

"But what's also exciting to me," Sarah continued, "is that I realize that I've already done a lot of what I'm describing in my current shop!

"The floors are the best oak. The ovens are the best you can buy. The display cases are absolutely gorgeous.

"My aunt would have loved my place.

"And that's what I also realized while I was thinking about all this. That if I'm ever in question about whether I'm doing it right or not, all I have to ask myself is, 'What would my aunt think?' and I'll know the answer.

"Can you see it?" she asked me honestly.

"Am I giving you a taste of what my Strategic Objective is? Am I being clear enough?"

"Sarah," I smiled, "you leave me speechless."

"Then, what's next?" she asked, as she poured each of us a fresh cup of tea.

14

YOUR ORGANIZATIONAL STRATEGY

All organizations are hierarchical. At each level people
serve under those above them. An organization is therefore
a structured institution. If it is not structured, it is a mob.
Mobs do not get things done, they destroy things.

Theodore Levitt
Management for Business Growth

Everyone wants to "get organized." But when you
suggest that they start by creating an Organization
Chart, all you get is doubtful—and sometimes hostile—
stares.

"Don't be ridiculous," a client once retorted. "We're
just a small company. We don't need an Organization
Chart. We need better people!"

Despite his protestations, I persisted.

Because I knew something he didn't.

I knew that the organizational development reflected
in the Organization Chart can have a more profound
impact on a small company than any other single Business Development step.

Organizing Around Personalities

Most companies organize around personalities rather than around functions.

That is, around people rather than accountabilities or responsibilities.

The result is almost always chaos.

To best show you what I mean, let's take a look at Widget Makers, a new company formed by Jack and Murray Hopeful, brothers and now partners, in an enterprise that they are sure will make them rich.

Jack and Murray start their partnership as most do, by sharing the work.

When Jack's not making the widget, Murray is.

When Jack's not helping the customer, Murray is.

When Murray's not doing the books, Jack is.

In the beginning, the business hums like a well-oiled machine.

The shop is spotless.

The windows gleam.

The floors are meticulous.

The customers smile.

And Jack and Murray hustle.

Taking turns, always taking turns.

On Monday, Murray opens up. On Tuesday, Jack. On Wednesday, Murray. On Thursday, Jack.

After all, they're partners aren't they?

If they don't do it, who will? It's only fair that they share the work.

And they go on that way. And the business begins to grow.

All of a sudden, there's more work than either Murray or Jack can handle. They have to get help.

So they hire Jerry. A great guy. And a nephew to boot.

As long as they have to pay someone, might as well keep it in the family.

Now it's Jack, Murray, and Jerry, taking turns, taking turns.

When Jack's not doing the books, Murray is.

And when Murray and Jack aren't, Jerry is.

Now when Murray isn't working with a customer, either Jack or Jerry is.

Or when Jack isn't opening up, Murray is, or Jerry.

Things are moving. The business is jumping. Jack and Murray and Jerry are as busy as three people can be.

It isn't long before Herb joins them. Jack's wife's brother. A good guy. A hard worker. Willing and eager.

Now it's Jack, Murray, Jerry, and Herb, taking turns, taking turns.

When Jack's not doing the books, Herb is, or Murray, or Jerry.

When Murray's not working with a customer, it's Jack or Jerry or Herb.

When Jerry's not making widgets, it's Murray or Jack or Herb.

Everybody's opening up, answering the telephone, going out for sandwiches, making deposits—taking turns, taking turns, taking turns.

But suddenly the widgets begin to come back. They don't seem to be working like they used to.

"We never had this trouble before," says Jack to Murray. Murray looks at Herb. Herb looks at Jerry.

All of a sudden, the books begin to look funny.

"We never had this trouble before," says Murray to

Jack. Jack looks at Jerry. Jerry looks at Herb.

And that's not all.

The shop is beginning to fall apart.

Tools are missing.

Dust is getting in the widgets.

Corrugated cardboard is strewn about the work table.

Nails are in the screw boxes and screws in the nail boxes.

Jack and Murray and Jerry and Herb are beginning to bump into each other on their way in and out.

They're elbowing for room in the work space.

Windows aren't getting cleaned.

Floors aren't getting swept.

Tempers begin to mount.

But who's to say something? And what? And to whom?

If everybody's doing everything, then who's accountable for anything?

If Jack and Murray are partners, who's in charge?

If both, then what happens when Jack tells Jerry to do something that Murray won't allow him to do?

When Herb wants to go for lunch, who does he tell— Jack? Murray? Jerry?

Who's accountable for making certain that the store is manned?

When the widgets go bad, who's accountable for correcting the condition?

When the books are unbalanced, who's accountable for balancing them?

When the floors need cleaning, when the windows need washing, when the shop needs opening or closing, when the customers need tending—who's accountable for producing the results?

What Jack and Murray don't understand is that without an Organization Chart, everything hinges on luck and good feelings, on the personalities of the people and the goodwill they share.

Unfortunately, personalities, good feelings, goodwill, and luck aren't the only ingredients of a successful organization; alone, they are the recipe for chaos and disaster.

Organization needs something more.

Organizing Your Company

Let's start Widget Makers all over again.

Jack and Murray Hopeful are sitting in their kitchen.

They have decided to form Widget Makers.

They are excited about its prospects but know that if it's to succeed they have to approach it differently from the way most people start a new business.

The first thing they decide to do is to think about the business as a corporation, rather than as a partnership.

Rather than thinking of themselves as partners, they now think of themselves as shareholders.

Having both worked in partnerships with other people—and failed—Jack and Murray know that there's nothing more disastrous than a partnership gone bad, as so many do.

Unless it's a family business, that is.

Jack and Murray already know that family businesses are even worse than partnerships.

But a partnership that's also a family business?

No. Jack and Murray decide to do it a different way.

Sitting there at the kitchen table, Jack and Murray each take a blank piece of paper and print their names at the top of the page.

Under each name they print "Primary Aim."

For the next hour or so, Jack and Murray each visualizes how he would like his life to look and writes his conclusions on the page in front of him.

Then they spend another hour or so talking about what they wrote, sharing their personal dreams with each other, perhaps discovering in that hour more about each other than they had known in all their years as brothers.

The next step Jack and Murray take is to draw a line across a blank piece of paper about a third of the way down. Above the line they write in bold letters the word **SHAREHOLDERS.** They have agreed with each other that is to be their role outside of the business.

Inside of the business, they have agreed, they will from this time forward think of themselves as **EMPLOYEES.**

They realize this will save them a lot of trouble later on.

The next step will require some time: the creation of the Strategic Objective for Widget Makers, Inc. Jack and Murray go at it enthusiastically. Murray agrees to do the necessary research concerning the Central Demographic Model they have tentatively chosen. How many potential buyers are there in the territory in which they've decided to do business? Is the population growing? What is the competition? How are widgets priced and how are they selling? Is there a future for widgets in the territory? What is the anticipated growth of the territory? Any zoning changes expected?

Murray also agrees to create a questionnaire and mail it to a sample of their Central Demographic Model consumers to find out how they feel they're treated by other widget companies. At the same time, Murray is to personally call 150 of those consumers. He'll conduct a Needs Analysis to get a better understanding of how they think and feel about widgets. What do widgets mean to them? How have widgets changed their lives? If they could have any kind of widget at all, what would it look like? How would it feel to use it? What do they want a good widget to do for them?

Murray agrees to do the research by a certain date.

Meanwhile, Jack agrees to pull together the preliminary financial data needed to secure a loan from the bank—an operating pro forma and a cash flow projection for the first year of operation.

Once the information about the consumer, the competition, and the pricing is collected, Jack and Murray will meet again and complete their Strategic Objective and plug in the final numbers needed for the loan.

Luck is with them. The information Murray collects about their Central Demographic Model, the competition, and the pricing is more than encouraging.

They complete their Strategic Objective and then begin the task of organizational development—the creation of their Organization Chart.

Since their Strategic Objective has indicated how they will be doing business (one location, assembling and selling widgets and widget-related accessories to a specific consumer within the territory described as North Marine West), Jack and Murray agree that their Organization Chart will require the following positions:

- President and Chief Operating Officer (COO), accountable for the overall achievement of the

Strategic Objective and reporting to the SHARE-HOLDERS who include, on an equal basis, Jack and Murray.

- Vice-President/Marketing, accountable for finding customers and finding new ways to provide customers with the satisfactions they derive from widgets, at lower cost, and with greater ease, and reporting to the COO.

- Vice-President/Operations, accountable for keeping customers by delivering to them what is promised by Marketing, and for discovering new ways of assembling widgets, at lower cost, and with greater efficiency so as to provide the customer with better service, reporting to the COO.

- Vice-President/Finance, accountable for supporting both Marketing and Operations in the fulfillment of their accountabilities by achieving the company's profitability standards, and by securing capital whenever it's needed, and at the best rates, also reporting to the COO.

- Reporting to the Vice-President/Marketing are two positions: Sales Manager and Advertising/Research Manager.

- Reporting to the Vice-President/Operations are three positions: Production Manager, Service Manager, and Facilities Manager.

- Reporting to the Vice-President/Finance are two positions: Accounts Receivable Manager and Accounts Payable Manager.

Jack and Murray sit back and look at the completed Organization Chart of Widget Makers, Inc., and smile. It sure looks like a big company. The only problem is that Jack and Murray's names will have to fill all the boxes! They're the only two employees.

But what they have effectively done is describe all the work that's going to be done in Widget Makers, Inc., when its full potential is realized.

More importantly, they have described the work that has to be done right away!

Jack and Murray realize that there's no difference between the Widget Makers of today and the Widget Makers of tomorrow; the work is the same; only the faces will change.

The next job Jack and Murray take on is writing a Position Contract for each position on their Organization Chart.

A Position Contract (as we call it at E-Myth Worldwide) is a summary of the results to be achieved by each position in the company, the work the occupant of that position is accountable for, a list of standards by which the results are to be evaluated, and a line for the signature of the person who agrees to fulfill those accountabilities.

Jack and Murray know that a Position Contract is not a job description.

It is a contract, rather than just a description, between the company and an employee, a summary of the rules of the company's game.

It provides each person in an organization with a sense of commitment and accountability.

Accountability literally means "stand up and be counted."

Therefore, the Position Contract is the document that identifies who's to stand up and what they're being counted on to produce.

Widget Makers, Inc.
Organization Chart

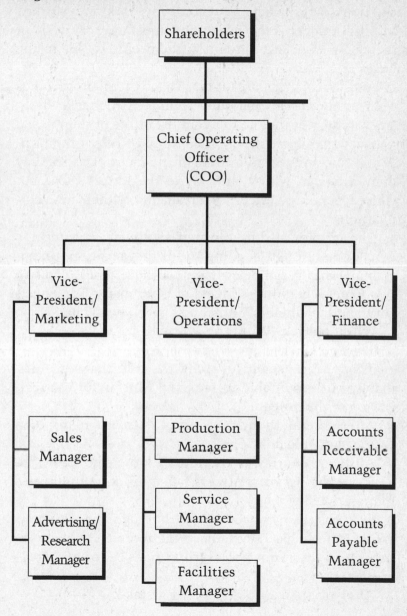

Having completed the Position Contracts for the positions within their new company, Jack and Murray, as shareholders, proceed to the most critical task of their new association: naming the people to put in the boxes.

And since there are only two of them, it becomes even more critical that they approach this task wisely and carefully, if they're to avoid the errors of their past.

Once they have that settled, they go below the horizontal line and in the middle of the piece of paper they draw a box in which they write the letters COO, for Chief Operating Officer, or President, of their new corporation.

The next most difficult step, of course, is to decide which one of them is going to fill that position, understanding that it can be only one of them. There can't be two Chief Operating Officers of a company. Someone's got to be accountable. Someone's got to be in charge.

Will it be Jack? Will it be Murray?

They ponder the question seriously.

This is the person fulfilling the role that will ultimately be accountable to Jack and Murray for the realization of their dream.

After careful thought, Murray decides on his own that Jack should do it.

Although Murray is the older brother, he knows in his heart that Jack has always taken his accountabilities more seriously.

Jack has always been more thorough than Murray. While Murray has always been the more creative of the two, creativity is not necessarily what's called for here— organization is.

After all, their life savings are at stake.

If the business is to give them both what they want, someone will have to take it very seriously indeed.

Murray confers with Jack about his decision.

They both understand what's at stake here. A commitment of trust, both to each other and to the Strategic Objective they have fashioned together with great care.

They both understand this is more than just a job: *it's a heartfelt commitment.*

After a long discussion, they agree on Jack for COO, and Jack solemnly accepts the position, as well as the authority that goes with it, by signing the Position Contract for COO, or President.

Next come the three Vice-Presidential positions: Marketing, Operations, and Finance.

Jack asks Murray if he would agree to be Vice-President/Marketing, since he did such an exceptional job on the marketing research project at the outset of their venture.

Murray agrees enthusiastically—this is the work he had hoped to do all along—and gladly signs the Vice-President/Marketing Position Contract. Jack then signs Murray's Position Contract as the President (the Vice-President/Marketing's manager) on behalf of the company.

Next comes Vice-President/Operations. Jack agrees to take this position because it will be difficult, he reasons with Murray, for Murray to both sell the widgets and make them at the same time. This time Jack signs the Position Contract both as Vice-President/Operations and as President.

Finally, Jack takes on the accountability of Vice-President/Finance, and signs the Position Contract for that position. There's no question between Jack and Murray who's best suited for that job.

Murray now assumes the positions of Sales Manager and Advertising/Research Manager, and signs those Position Contracts.

Jack takes the positions of Production Manager, Service Manager, and Facilities Manager, as well as those of Accounts Payable Manager and Accounts Receivable Manager, and signs those Position Contracts.

With all Position Contracts signed, Jack and Murray sit back for a second time to survey what they've done. When they see it, they're shocked! Jack has been given eight jobs to Murray's three! Something's got to be changed.

After some thought, they agree to have Murray take on the accountabilities of Accounts Receivable and Accounts Payable as well as that of Service Manager.

That makes it six jobs each.

Anyone should be able to do six jobs on an average day, Jack and Murray think to themselves ambitiously.

And, finally, the organization is done!

Not a bit of work had been performed on the job, and yet the two of them were able to conceive of the company, the work that needs to be done, the standards by which they would hold each position accountable, and which position is accountable to which position and specifically for what.

And upon completing this one preparatory act, a sense of order swept through Jack and Murray. A sense of elation.

For despite the obvious size of the job ahead, somehow it looked doable.

Somehow Jack and Murray knew they were going to get it all done.

They were organized.

They had some semblance of a plan.

In creating their Organization Chart, Jack and Murray had also generated the blueprint for their Franchise Prototype.

Prototyping the Position: Replacing Yourself with a System

Having created a picture of the business as it will look when it's finally done, Jack and Murray start the prototyping process.

But at the *bottom* of the organization, not at the top.

They start working on the business where they start working in the business.

In the position of Salesperson and Production Person and Accounts Receivable Clerk.

Not as the owners or partners or shareholders. Not as the COO or the VP/Marketing.

But as *employees*, at the very bottom of the organization. Doing Tactical Work, not Strategic Work.

Tactical Work is the work all technicians do.

Strategic Work is the work their managers do.

If Jack and Murray's business is going to thrive, they have to find other people to do the Tactical Work so as to free Jack and Murray to do the Strategic Work.

The Organization Chart is the means through which that critical transition can be made.

Let's watch as Jack and Murray go through the same growth process they experienced at the beginning of this chapter, but this time avoiding their earlier disaster by prototyping the positions in their Organization Chart.

Jack and Murray go to work in their business. But now with a difference. They are no longer interested in *working in their business.* They are now focused on *developing a business that works.* To do that they begin to work in an entirely different way.

As Murray goes to work *in* the position of Salesperson, he also goes to work *on* the position of Salesperson as Vice-President/Marketing.

As Jack goes to work *in* the position of Production Person, he also goes to work *on* the position of Production Person as Vice-President/Operations.

In other words, Murray and Jack start building their business by looking at each position in the business *as though it were a Franchise Prototype of its own.*

As Murray goes to work *in* the position of Salesperson as a Salesperson, he also goes to work *on* the position of Salesperson by implementing the Business Development Process of Innovation, Quantification, and Orchestration.

Likewise, when Jack goes to work *in* the position of Production Person as a Production Person, he goes to work *on* the position of Production Person by implementing the Business Development Process of Innovation, Quantification, and Orchestration.

Each of them asks, "What would best serve our customer here? How could I most easily give the customer what he wants while also maximizing profits for the company? And at the same time, how could I give the person responsible for that work the best possible experience?"

Murray begins to test the clothing he wears as a Salesperson to see what colors and styles produce the greatest positive impact on the customers.

He starts testing different words.

He begins to think about how Widget Makers, Inc., interacts with its customers, and how each component of this interaction could be modified to increase its effectiveness.

And as he quantifies the impact of his innovations on sales, he takes the most productive of them and writes them down in the *Widget Makers Sales Operations Manual.*

Before long, the *Sales Operations Manual* contains the exact scripts for handling incoming calls, outgoing calls, meeting the customer at the door. The exact responses to customer inquiries, complaints, concerns. The system by which an order is entered, returns are transacted, new product requests are acted upon, inventory is secured.

Only when the *Sales Operations Manual* is complete does Murray run an ad for a salesperson.

But not for someone with sales experience.

Not a Master Technician. But a novice. A beginner. An Apprentice.

Someone eager to learn how to do it right.

Someone willing to learn what Murray has spent so much time and energy discovering.

Someone for whom questions haven't become answers.

Someone who is open to the possibility of learning skills he hasn't developed yet, skills he wants to learn.

And the ad is placed under Sales in the Classified Section of the Sunday paper. It reads: COME AND SEE OUR TURN-KEY OPERATION. COME AND SEE OUR MONEY MACHINE. NO EXPERIENCE NECESSARY. JUST AN OPEN MIND AND A WILLINGNESS TO LEARN.

And as Murray interviews the candidates, he shows them the *Sales Operations Manual* and Widget Makers'

Strategic Objective, and explains how they were created and why.

He tells them the story of Widget Makers, the dream he and Jack conceived, to enable them to make a personal difference in the market in which they have chosen to become leaders.

He shows them the Organization Chart, where the position of Salesperson is, to which position it reports, and who in Widget Makers is currently accountable for that position.

He talks to them about their Primary Aim to determine who among them has a vision that coincides with Widget Makers' view of the world.

And when he finds the right person, Murray hires him, hands him the *Sales Operations Manual*, has him memorize the words in it, dress to code, learn the systems, and finally, go to work. *Using the Sales System, Murray innovated, quantified, and orchestrated.*

At that moment, at that exact instant, Murray moves up to the position of Sales Manager *and begins the process of Business Development all over again.*

Because at that moment, Murray has taken the most important step in freeing himself from the Tactical Work of his business. Murray has replaced himself with a *system* that works in the hands of a person who wants to work it.

And now Murray's job becomes managing the system rather than doing the work.

Murray is now engaged in Strategic Work.

And while Murray did that, Jack did the very same thing for each of the Tactical Work positions he was responsible for!

Both of them working on the business while working in it, and all according to plan.

Now Jack and Murray have learned, by experience, an important lesson in developing their business, a lesson every Technician suffering from an Entrepreneurial Seizure must learn if his business and his life are to work in harmony.

That your Organization Chart flows down from your Strategic Objective, which in turn flows down from your Primary Aim.

That each is the cause of the one preceding it, and each, therefore, plays a part in the fulfillment of the one before it.

A logic is established, an integrated whole.

In this example, Widget Makers, Inc., became an orderly system for creating and re-creating Jack and Murray's lives.

Without the Organization Chart, confusion, discord, and conflict become the order of the day.

But with it, the direction, purpose, and style of the business are balanced, interacting purposefully and progressing with intention and integrity toward a cohesive and sensible whole.

Finally, good people could come together and get something done!

Sarah exhaled loudly and stretched, both arms extending fully toward the ceiling as though she was letting go of a feeling she was having difficulty handling.

"Boy," she said, "you sure don't make it easy. The minute I think I've got this entrepreneurial thing handled, you give me some more work to do.

"I'd like to go back over this again because I'm not sure I've got it.

"What you're saying is that I need to create an Organization Chart for All About Pies as it will look when it's done, seven years from now, rather than the way it is now?"

"Yes," I responded.

"And that once I've created that Organization Chart, I need to put my name in all the positions I currently fill?"

"Right again," I answered.

"And that I need to create very detailed descriptions of each one of those positions, and then sign the Position Contracts for each, as though I were an employee taking responsibility for each job? Do you mean I actually need to sign each Position Contract, exactly as though I were that employee?"

"Yes," I said, "exactly as though you were that employee. Because if your business is going to work, you are each one of those employees! Until you replace yourself with someone else, that is."

She continued to press forward, her eyes shining like diamonds, intense, awake, engaged.

"And the reason for that is," Sarah said, "that unless I act as I expect my employees to act, unless I work in my business exactly as I wish them to, I will never be able to create a system for doing it exactly the way I expect them to do it.

"In other words, unless I act in exactly the same way as I expect my employees to act, the system I create will indulge my preferences, rather than what the business really needs to make it possible for everyone other than me to be as productive and happy as possible.

"And if I only indulge my preferences, I will never be able to replace myself with anyone other than another owner, someone just like me, someone with the same interests as an owner, someone with the same goals as mine."

She paused for a moment as though to catch her breath, and then added, "Is that what you are saying?"

"Exactly!" I answered. "Because it's critical if you are to begin your business all over again that you're able to separate yourself from the roles you need to play. To become independent of them, rather than these roles becoming dependent on you.

"Remember we talked earlier about the crazy-making nature of all your different personalities, and that the only way to eliminate that craziness is to organize yourself and the world around you as clearly as possible so you can function as clearly as possible?

"Well, it's the dysfunctional nature of these unconscious personalities we have to combat.

"It's our automatic nature we've got to organize into an intentional nature.

"And the only way we can do that is intentionally, not automatically.

"And so one part of us, the part a man named Gurdjieff once called the 'driver,' must order all the rest.

"The driver must take charge of the horse and carriage, Gurdjieff once said.

"And, as the owner of your business, as the driver of your business, that's your primary job: to take charge of the horse and carriage.

"And, to do so, you must be able to differentiate among all the roles, to discriminate between what's most important and what's least important, to organize it in such a way that your best intelligence tells you your business must work.

"And, once you have done that, once you've organized your business in the most intelligent way you can, your next most important job is to follow the rules of the game you have created with integrity.

"Because if you won't follow the rules, why should anyone else?

"If the rules don't apply to you, the leader, why should you expect anyone to follow you?

"If you don't obey the rules, honor them, extol them, why should you expect anyone else to take your game seriously?

"The answer is, you can't expect them to, because they won't!

"And that's what this whole process of organizational development is. It's the process through which you think through your business as best as you're able and then structure the way it is to work. Your Organization Chart is that structure. It is you talking to your people and the world, telling them exactly how you see your business working when it's done. When the dream is in place. It's you sharing your mind with the world. And then, once having shared it, it's you telling your people and the world that you believe enough in the vision to live it yourself!

"Anything less than that is sheer arrogance," I told her.

"But, when you live by your own rules, when you 'walk your talk,' when you live as you think, then your business will become a thing to behold."

"Got it!" she said.

"I didn't have a doubt in the world but you would," I responded.

"So, let's go on to Management Development," I said to Sarah, as I poured her a fresh cup of tea, "and then to People Development.

"Because where management, people, and systems come together, so does your Prototype."

15

YOUR MANAGEMENT STRATEGY

The System is the Solution.

AT&T

You may think that the successful implementation of a management strategy is dependent on finding amazingly competent managers—people with finely honed "people skills," with degrees from management schools, with highly sophisticated techniques for dealing with and developing their people.

It isn't.

You don't need such people.

Nor can you afford them.

In fact, they will be the bane of your existence.

What you need, instead, is a Management System.

The *System* will become your management strategy, the means through which your Franchise Prototype produces the results you want.

The *System* will become your solution to the problems that beset you because of the unpredictability of your people.

The *System* will transform your people problems

into an opportunity by orchestrating the process by which management decisions are made while eliminating the need for such decisions wherever and whenever possible.

What Is a Management System?

It is a System designed into your Prototype to produce a marketing result.

And the more automatic that System is, the more effective your Franchise Prototype will be.

Management Development—the process through which you create your Management System, and teach your up-and-coming managers to use it—isn't a management tool as many people believe. It's a *marketing* tool.

Its purpose is not just to create an efficient Prototype but an effective one.

And an effective Prototype is a business that finds and keeps customers—profitably—better than any other.

Let's look at how such a system was put into practice by a resort hotel I've patronized over the past seventeen years.

A Match, a Mint, a Cup of Coffee, and a Newspaper

The first time it was an accident; that is, an accident for me. I hadn't planned to go there.

I'd been driving for seven hours, and, tired of the road, decided to stop for the night before going on to San Francisco.

The hotel was located in a redwood grove overlooking the Pacific.

By the time I walked into the lobby, the sun was setting and the grove had turned dark as pitch.

Instantly something told me that I was in a special place. The lobby was warmly lighted. Redwood paneling reflected the red glow of the light onto beige over-stuffed couches that hugged the three walls surrounding the reception desk. A long, dark wood table faced the front door through which I had just entered. On the table rested a huge woven Indian basket overflowing with fresh fruit. Beside the basket stood a massive bronze lamp, its deep burnished light bouncing off the fruit, adding a festive look to the room. Running the full length of the table and falling down on either end almost to the floor was an intricately crocheted linen cloth, its bright, exotic pattern accentuating the colors of the fruit, the bronze of the lamp, and the deep red ochre of the walls.

At the far side of the table, against the far wall, in a massive fieldstone fireplace, a roaring fire filled the room with the cheerful crackling of its furiously burning oak logs.

Even if I hadn't been so tired, the contrast between the heat of the flames on my face and the cold of the night at my back would have been enough to attract me to the room. As it was, I practically melted with delight.

Behind the reception desk a woman appeared dressed in a freshly starched red, green, and white gingham blouse and a deep red ochre skirt. A pin with the logo of the hotel atop a red ochre ribbon decorated her blouse like a badge of honor. A matching ribbon held her hair back from a glowing face.

"Welcome to Venetia," she smiled warmly.

It took no more than three minutes from the moment she spoke that greeting to the time the bellboy ushered me into my room, despite the fact that I had no reservation. I couldn't believe the ease with which it all happened.

And the room! The overall impression was one of understated opulence—thick, muted pastel wall-to-wall carpeting; a four-poster, king-size white pine bed covered by a magnificent, impeccably clean, white-on-white quilt; original graphics depicting scenes and birds of the Pacific Northwest gracing the rough-hewn elegance of the natural cedar walls; a stone fireplace with oak logs already prepared and waiting on the grate for the fire someone knew I would appreciate, paper rolled ceremoniously beneath the grate, and an elegant oversized match lying diagonally across the hearth, waiting to be struck.

Delighted with my good fortune, I changed for dinner; the woman at the desk had made my reservation when she checked me in! I walked out into the night to find the restaurant. A sign by a path outside of my room pointed me down another well-lit path through the dark redwood grove.

The night air was still and clear.

In the distance I could hear the hushed, rhythmic patter of the Pacific Ocean surf. Or was it my imagination? It scarcely mattered; an aura of magic surrounded the place.

The restaurant stood on a knoll overlooking the hotel and the ocean. Until I went inside, I hadn't seen another person, but the restaurant was crowded.

I gave the maitre d' my name and he immediately showed me to a table, despite the fact that other people were waiting. Evidently, reservations meant something in this restaurant!

The meal was as delightful as everything I had experienced before it, the food attractively prepared, the service attentive yet unobtrusive. I lingered over a glass of brandy while enjoying a classical guitarist who played a selection of Bach fugues for the dinner guests.

I signed the check and returned to my room, noting on the way that the lights had been turned up on the path apparently to compensate for the growing darkness.

By the time I arrived at my room, the night had become chilly. I was looking forward to a fire and possibly another brandy before going to bed.

Somebody had beaten me to it!

A brisk fire was burning in the fireplace. The quilt was turned down on the bed. The pillows were plumped up, a mint resting on each one.

On one of the night tables beside the bed stood a glass of brandy and a card. I picked up the card and read:

> *Welcome to your first stay at Venetia. I hope it has been enjoyable. If there is anything I can do for you, day or night, please don't hesitate to call.*
> *Kathi*

As I drifted to sleep that evening, I felt very well taken care of.

The following morning I awoke to a strange bubbling sound in the bathroom. I arose to investigate.

A pot of coffee, turned on by an automatic timer, was merrily perking away on the sink counter. A card resting against the pot said:

> *Your brand of coffee. Enjoy! K.*

And it *was* my brand of coffee!

How in the world could they have known that?

And then I remembered. At the restaurant the night before they had asked me what brand of coffee I preferred. And here it was!

Just as I caught on to what they had done, there was a polite knock at the door.

I went to the door and opened it. Nobody. But there on the mat was a newspaper. My newspaper, the *New York Times*.

How in the world did they know that?

And then I remembered. When I checked in the night before the receptionist had asked me what newspaper I preferred. I hadn't given it another thought. Until now. And there it was!

And exactly the same scenario has occurred each and every time I've returned.

But after that first time I was never asked my preferences again.

I had become a part of the hotel's Management System.

And never once has it let me down.

The system knows what I like and makes certain that I get it, in exactly the same way, at exactly the same time.

What exactly had the System provided? A match, a mint, a cup of coffee, and a newspaper!

But it wasn't the match, the mint, the cup of coffee, or the newspaper that did it. *It was that somebody had heard me.*

And they heard me *every single time*!

The moment I walked into the room and felt the fire, I knew that someone had thought about me. Had thought about what *I* wanted.

I hadn't said a word, and yet they had heard me.

The moment I saw the mints on the pillows, the

turned-down quilt, and the brandy on the table, I knew that someone had thought about me. Had thought about what I wanted.

I hadn't said a word and yet they had heard me.

The moment I heard the coffee pot perking in the bathroom and saw the card that identified it as my brand, I remembered that someone had asked for my preference.

And they had heard my answer.

The instant I saw the newspaper and recognized it as my newspaper, I remembered that someone had asked.

And they had heard my answer.

And it was totally automatic!

Every single element was an orchestrated solution designed to produce a marketing result, an integrated component of the hotel's Management System.

After my third visit to the hotel, I asked to speak with the Manager.

I wanted to find out how he was able to produce the identical results for me every single time.

How could he make certain that someone would ask the right questions so as to ensure the correct results for each and every guest?

Was it because he hired extremely competent people?

Were the employees owners?

Was it some kind of special incentive system?

The Manager was a young man of twenty-nine. He invited me into his office to talk. It was well-lit, modest in size, and overlooked the redwood grove I had walked through to get to the restaurant. His desk was clean and neatly organized, not a loose paper in sight.

"This is a very orderly young man," I thought to myself.

"Perhaps *he's* the reason the hotel works so well."

The young Manager obviously enjoyed his job, because he warmed immediately to the conversation about his work and the task of producing the results for which he was held accountable by the hotel's owner.

"You know," he said, smiling self-consciously, "it's funny sitting here talking to you about what we do here at the hotel. Because until five months ago, the only experience I had in the hotel business was as a guest for two nights at a Holiday Inn in Fresno three years ago.

"In fact," he continued, "before this job I was working as a short-order cook at a restaurant nearby. The owner and I got to know each other. He asked if I'd like to learn the hotel business, and, before I knew it, he hired me. Everything I know about the hotel business I've learned here.

"Here, let me show you."

He reached behind his desk for a red binder. Printed on the spine were the initials OM and the logo of the hotel.

"What we do here is simple. Anyone can do it."

He opened the binder to the table of contents.

"This is our *Operations Manual.* As you can see, it's nothing but a series of checklists. This one is a checklist for setting up a room." He opened the book to a yellow page.

"This group of pages is yellow. Everything in the *Manual* is color coded. Yellow has to do with Room Setup. Blue, with Guest Support Services. For instance, when we light your fire at night, put the mints on your pillow, and so on.

"Each checklist itemizes the specific steps each Room Support Person must take to do his or her job.

There are eight packages of checklists for each Room Support Person waiting in their mailbox when they come in every day. Each package of checklists is used for one of the eight rooms the Room Support Person is accountable for.

"As a Room Support Person goes about the process of taking care of his or her eight rooms, a checklist is completed to confirm that each accountability was performed according to the standards. As you can see, here at the bottom of the checklist is a place for the RSP to sign, indicating that he or she did the prescribed work.

"To sign and not to have done the work is grounds for instant dismissal.

"But there's another part of the system that really makes it work.

"On the back of each checklist is a drawing of the specific room that identifies each task to be completed, and the order in which it has to be done. The drawing takes the RSP through the routine, and, as they complete each task, they check off the corresponding part of the drawing to show that it was done.

"With this drawing we can train new people almost instantly and have them producing a result identical to that of a person who's been with us for quite some time.

"As added insurance, my RSP Supervisors run spot checks every day to make certain that any errors are caught in time."

He paused and smiled. "But there are rarely any errors. The system works like a charm.

"There's an equally effective system for everything we do here. The fact is, the owner worked it all out in advance. The lighting, the sauna, and the pool are timed electronically and synchronized with the seasons, so that they deliver a predictable result to the guests. For example, you might have noticed that at night the outdoor lights increase in intensity as it gets darker. That's done automatically. No one has to think about it.

"I could give you lots of other examples, but I think you get the point. The whole thing was put together in a way the owner believed would make a positive impression on our guests. You'd be amazed at how many people come up to me after staying here just to thank me for how well they were treated.

"But it's not the big things they talk about; it's always the little things."

I could understand and believe all he had said, but still I asked, "How do you get your RSPs to use the checklists? How do you get them to use the system? Don't they get tired of the routine? Doesn't it get boring for them?"

"Ah," said my willing host.

"That's where we *really* shine."

16

YOUR PEOPLE STRATEGY

Life games reflect life aims.

Robert S. DeRopp
The Master Game

"How do I get my people to do what I want?" This is the one question I hear most often from small business owners.

And the answer I invariably give them is, "You can't! You can't get your people to do anything.

"If you want it done," I tell them, "you're going to have to create an environment in which 'doing it' is more important to your people than not doing it. Where 'doing it' well becomes a way of life for them."

Since that is the question most often asked of me, I was intrigued with the hotel Manager's answer to my question, "How do you get your people to do what you want?"

His response was refreshing because it is so rare that I hear something like it.

"The first thing that surprised me when I came to work here," the Manager said, "was that the owner took me seriously.

"I mean, think about it. Here I was, a kid, with absolutely no experience in this business. But he never treated me that way. He treated me as though I were a serious adult. Somebody worth talking to about what he obviously considered important.

"And that was the second thing that surprised me when I came to work here," the Manager continued. "How seriously the Boss took the operation of this hotel.

"I mean, it wasn't just that he took it seriously—everyone I've ever worked for was serious about his business—it was the *kind* of seriousness he had.

"It was as though the hotel was more than just a hotel to him.

"It was like the hotel was an expression of who he was, a symbol of what he believed in.

"So if I hadn't taken the hotel seriously, it would have looked like I wasn't taking him seriously, as a man whose values I respected.

"I guess that's why he took me seriously. It established a level of communication between us that made it possible for me to listen to what he believed in and how the hotel expressed those beliefs on a day-to-day basis.

"I'll never forget my first day here," he went on. "It was like I was being initiated into a fraternity or something.

"It was right here that it happened." He waved his arm in a circle indicating the office in which we were sitting. "This used to bc his office.

"I was sitting where you're sitting," he said. "And the Boss was sitting here." He pointed at the chair in which he was sitting.

"It was a Monday morning and they had just had a

big weekend, so there was a ton of stuff to do. Usually when I start a new job, the first thing that happens is that the person who hires me takes a minute to describe what I'm supposed to do and then throws me out there to do it. So I was surprised when the Boss asked me if I wanted a cup of coffee. He seemed so unhurried, so unbusinesslike, you might say.

"No that wasn't it," the Manager corrected himself.

"He was probably the most businesslike person I had ever met.

"But it was *how* he was about his business that struck me.

"He seemed to be saying that what we were going to talk about was the most important thing on his agenda that day, that discussing my job was more important to him than doing the work that was going on at the time.

"He wasn't hiring me to *work;* he was hiring me to do something much more important than that."

The Manager smiled. "You know, I've never said this to anyone before. It's really strange, but while I'm telling you all of this, it's becoming clear to me why I have so much respect for this place. It's because I have so much respect for the Boss. To me, the place is him. If I didn't respect him, I don't think I would be as good at what I do here as I am. Somehow the *idea* of what we do here is his idea. And that's what he took so long to communicate to me on that first day—his idea of this place. And what that meant to him.

"What he told me was something nobody has ever said to me before in any job.

"He said, 'The work we do is a reflection of who we are. If we're sloppy at it, it's because we're sloppy inside. If we're late at it, it's because we're late inside. If we're bored by it, it's because we're bored inside, with ourselves, not with the work. The most menial work can be a piece of art when done by an artist. So the job here is not outside of ourselves, but inside of ourselves. How we do our work becomes a mirror of how we are inside.' "

The Manager continued, as if the owner were talking through him. "Work is passive without you. It can't do anything. Work is only an idea before a person does it. But the moment a person does it, the impact of the work on the world becomes a reflection of that idea—the idea behind the work—as well as the person doing it.

"In the process, the work you do becomes you. And you become the force that breathes life into the idea behind the work.

"You become the creator of the impact on the world of the work you do.

"There is no such thing as undesirable work," he continued. "There are only people who see certain kinds of work as undesirable. People who use every excuse in the world to justify why they have to do work they hate to do. People who look upon their work as a punishment for who they are and where they stand in the world, rather than as an opportunity to see themselves as they really are.

"What the Boss said is that people like that don't bring life to the idea of the work they do; they bring death to it.

"The result of that is always what we experience as the sloppy, inconsiderate, inconsistent, and inhuman transactions that take place between most businesses and the people who buy from them. Exactly the opposite of what we have here.

"And the reason it's different here is because we give

everyone who comes to work at the hotel an opportunity to make a choice. Not after they've done the work, but before.

"And we do that *by making sure they understand the idea behind the work they're being asked to do.*

"I guess that's what excited me most about taking this job," said the Manager. "It's the very first place I've ever gone to work where *there was an idea behind the work that was more important than the work itself.*

"The idea the Boss expressed to me was broken down into three parts:

"The first says that the customer is not always right, but whether he is or not, it is our job to make him feel that way.

"The second says that everyone who works here is expected to work toward being the best he can possibly be at the tasks he's accountable for. When he can't do that, he should act like he is until he gets around to it. And if he's unwilling to act like it, he should leave.

"The third says that the business is a place where everything we know how to do is tested by what we don't know how to do, and that the conflict between the two is what creates growth, what creates meaning.

"The idea the Boss has about the business comes down to one essential notion. That a business is like a martial arts practice hall, a *dojo*, a place you go to practice being the best you can be. But the true combat in a dojo is not between one person and another as most people believe it to be. The true combat in a martial arts practice hall is between the people *within ourselves.*

"That's what the Boss and I talked about in our first meeting. His philosophy about work and about business. I came to understand that the hotel was the least important thing in our relationship. What was important was how seriously I took to playing the game he had created here.

"He wasn't looking for employees so much as for players in his game. He was looking for people who wanted something more than just a job."

What the Manager was telling me, and what the Boss had told him, was that people—your people—do not simply want to work for exciting people. They want to work for people who have created a clearly defined structure for acting in the world. A structure through which they can test themselves and be tested. Such a structure is called a game.

And there is nothing more exciting than a well-conceived game.

That is what the very best businesses represent to the people who create them: a game to be played in which the rules symbolize the idea you, the owner, have about the world.

If your idea is a positive one, your business will reflect that optimism.

If your idea is a negative one, your business will reflect that as well.

In this context, the degree to which your people "do what you want" is the degree to which they buy into your game.

And the degree to which they buy into your game doesn't depend on them but on how well you communicate the game to them—at the *outset* of your relationship, not after it's begun.

Your People Strategy is the way you communicate this idea.

It starts with your Primary Aim and your Strategic

Objective, and continues through your Organizational Strategy (your Organization Chart and the Position Contracts for all of the positions in it) and the *Operations Manuals* that define the work your people do.

It is communicated through the beliefs you have and the way you expect your Prototype to exemplify them; through the standards you establish for the performance of accountabilities at all levels and in all sectors of your Prototype; through the words you use to describe what your business needs to become—for your customer, for your people, for yourself—if it is to be more than just a place where people go to work.

But the game your business will play can't simply be captured on the written page. It must be seen if it is to work. It must be experienced.

It is—first, last, and always—about *how you act*.

The words will become hollow if the game is a contrived one.

The game can't be created as a device to enroll your people. It can't become cynical if it's to provide your people with what they need in order to come alive while playing it.

The game has to be real. You have to mean it.

The game is a measure of you.

How you act in the game establishes how you will be regarded by the other players.

The Rules of the Game

As in any game, the "people game" has rules that must be honored if you are to become any good at it.

I've included a few here to give you a taste for them. As for the rest of them, you'll have to discover them for

yourself by playing a game of your own. You'll learn the
rules in the process.

1. **Never figure out what you want your people to do
   and then try to create a game out of it.** If it's to be
   seen as serious, the game has to come first; what
   your people do, second.
2. **Never create a game for your people you're
   unwilling to play yourself.** They'll find you out
   and never let you forget it.
3. **Make sure there are specific ways of winning the
   game without ending it.** The game can never end
   because the end will take the life right out of your
   business. But unless there are victories in the process, your people will grow weary. Hence, the
   value of victories now and then. They keep people
   in the game and make the game appealing, even
   when it's not.
4. **Change the game from time to time—the tactics,
   not the strategy.** The strategy is its ethic, the
   moral underpinning of your game's logic. This
   must remain sacrosanct, for it is the foundation of
   you and your people's commitment to each other.
   But change is necessary. For any game can
   become ordinary, no matter how exhilarating it
   may be at the beginning.
     To know when change is called for, watch your
   people. Their results will tell you when the
   game's all but over. The trick is to anticipate the
   end before anyone else does and to change it by
   executive action. You'll know if you've pulled it
   off by watching how everyone responds to the
   change. Not at first, however. You can expect some

resistance at first. But persist. Your persistence will move them through their resistance into your new and more enlivening game.

5. **Never expect the game to be self-sustaining. People need to be reminded of it constantly.** At least once a week, create a special meeting about the game. At least once a day, make some kind of issue about an exception to the way the game has been played—and make certain that everyone knows about it.

Remember, in and of itself the game doesn't exist. It is alive to the degree that people make it so. But people have the unerring ability to forget everything they start and to be distracted by trivia. Most great games are lost that way. To make certain yours isn't, don't expect your people to be something they're not. Remind them, time after time, of the game they're playing with you. You can't remind them too often.

6. **The game has to make sense.** An illogical game will abort before it ever gets going. The best games are built on universally verifiable truths. Everyone should be able to see them if they're to be sufficiently attractive. A game with muddy beginnings will get you nowhere. Know the ground you stand on and then assemble your armament. Sooner or later you'll need it. For a game that isn't tested isn't a game at all.

But remember, you can have the best reasons in the world for your game and still end up with a loser if the logic is not supported by a strong emotional commitment. All the logic does is give your people the rational armament to support

their emotional commitment. If their commitment wanes, it means that they—and most
likely, you—have forgotten the logic. So wheel
out the logic often. Make sure everyone remem-
bers the game's raison d'être.

7. **The game needs to be fun from time to time.**
Note that I said, *from time to time.* No game
needs to be fun all the time. In fact, a game is
often no fun at all. That's part of the thrill of playing a game well: learning how to deal with the
"no fun" part so as to retain your dignity while
falling on your face.

At the same time, fun needs to be planned into
your game. But make certain that the fun you
plan *is* fun. Fun needs to be defined by your people. If it's fun to them, it will work. But not too
often, maybe once every six months. Something
to look forward to, and something to forget.

8. **If you can't think of a good game, steal one.** Anyone's ideas are as good as your own. But once you
steal somebody else's game, learn it by heart.
There's nothing worse than pretending to play a
game.

The Logic of the Game

To the hotel Manager, the Boss's game was a good
one, so he learned how to play it. It was a simple game,
but effective. It was built on the following logic:

Most people today are not getting what they want.
Not from their jobs, not from their families, not from
their religion, not from their government, and, most
important, not from themselves.

Something is missing in most of our lives.

Part of what's missing is purpose. Values. Worthwhile standards against which our lives can be measured. Part of what's missing is a *Game Worth Playing*.

What's also missing is a sense of relationship.

People suffer in isolation from one another.

In a world without purpose, without meaningful values, what have we to share but our emptiness, the needy fragments of our superficial selves?

As a result, most of us scramble about hungrily seeking distraction, in music, in television, in people, in drugs.

And most of all we seek things.

Things to wear and things to do.

Things to fill the emptiness.

Things to shore up our eroding sense of self.

Things to which we can attach meaning, significance, life.

We've fast become a world of things. And most people are being buried in the profusion.

What most people need, then, is a place of community that has purpose, order, and meaning.

A place in which *being* human is a prerequisite, but *acting* human is essential.

A place where the generally disorganized thinking that pervades our culture becomes organized and clearly focused on a specific worthwhile result.

A place where discipline and will become prized for what they are: the backbone of enterprise and action, of being what you are intentionally instead of accidentally.

A place that replaces the home most of us have lost.

That's what a business can do; it can create a *Game Worth Playing*.

It can become that place of community.

It can become that place where words such as

integrity, intention, commitment, vision, and *excellence* can be used as action steps in the process of producing a worthwhile result.

What kind of result?

Giving your customer a sense that your business is a special place, created by special people, doing what they do in the best possible way.

And all being done for the simplest, most human reason possible—because they're alive!

What other reason do you need?

Human beings are capable of performing extraordinary acts. Capable of going to the moon. Capable of creating the computer. Capable of building a bomb that can destroy us all.

The least we should be able to do is run a small business that works.

For if we can't do that, then what's the value of our grand ideas?

What purpose do they serve but to alienate us from ourselves, from each other, from who we are?

Playing the Game

Thinking the way the hotel owner did, you can begin to construct a mental map of the game he created. His hotel became a world in which the sensory experiences of his customer were greeted by a profound dedication to cleanliness, beauty, and order.

But this dedication didn't rest on a purely commercial justification (though there was that too; no business could be successful without it) but a moral one. On the Boss's philosophy, his view of the world, his idea.

The idea was then communicated to his people, both

in word and deed, through a well-planned process.

The importance of this cannot be overstated.

The Boss communicated his idea through documented systems and through his warm, moving, and positive manner.

He knew that he could communicate the orderly yet human process of pleasing customers to his people only if it were communicated to them in an orderly and human way.

In short, the *medium* of communication became as important as the idea it was designed to communicate.

And the hotel's hiring process became the first and most essential medium for communicating the Boss's idea.

As the Manager explained it to me, the hiring process was comprised of several distinct components:

1. A scripted presentation communicating the Boss's idea in a group meeting to all of the applicants at the same time. This presentation described not only the idea but also the business's history and experience in successfully implementing that idea, and the attributes required of the successful candidate for the position in question.
2. Meeting with each applicant individually to discuss his reactions to and feelings about the idea, as well as his background and experience. At this meeting, each applicant was also asked why he felt he was superbly appropriate for the role the position was to play in implementing the Boss's idea.
3. Notification of the successful candidate by telephone. Again, a scripted presentation.

4. Notification of the unsuccessful applicants, thanking each for his interest. A standard letter, signed by the interviewer.

5. First day of training to include the following activities for both the Boss and the new employee:

- Reviewing the Boss's idea
- Summarizing the system through which the entire business brings the idea to reality
- Taking the new employee on a tour of the facilities, highlighting people at work and systems at work to demonstrate the interdependence of the systems on people and the people on systems
- Answering clearly and fully all the employee's questions
- Issuing the employee his uniform and his *Operations Manual*
- Reviewing the *Operations Manual*, including the Strategic Objective, the Organizational Strategy, and the Position Contract of the employee's position
- Completing the employment papers

And the hiring process is just the beginning!

Just think. All of this simply to *start* a relationship!

Are you beginning to understand that systematizing your business need not be a dehumanizing experience, but quite the opposite?

That in order to get your people to do what you want, you'll first have to create an environment that will make it possible?

That hiring people, developing people, and keeping people requires a strategy built on an understanding of people completely foreign to most businesses?

That the system is indeed the solution?

That without an idea worth pursuing, there can be no People Strategy at all?

But with that idea you can finally say, just as our young Manager said, "That's where we really shine!"

Management, people, systems. As I watched Sarah take all this in, I saw that the idea of this integrated view of business had begun to take hold of her imagination.

Gone was the resistance, the doubt, and the fear that what I had brought to her door was beyond her, something unreachable for the baker of pies she had come to believe she was.

What she was beginning to grasp is that she was a worthy opponent, more worthy than she had ever realized, and that the game I was describing for her was the same game she had been taught to play by her aunt, years ago in her mother's kitchen, with such loving attention. That there was absolutely no difference!

She smiled at me, as though reading my thoughts.

"I'm beginning to see the connection between all these things we've talked about," she said. "They're all beginning to make sense. The puzzle is coming together. I can see the parts merge into an exciting picture that I now know has been there all along! All that needed to be done for the picture to take form was for someone to move the pieces into their proper place. I'd like to describe it for you, the picture I'm beginning to see, before I ask you some more questions."

"Go right ahead," I smiled. "In fact, I'd be disappointed if you didn't."

"It all goes back to my childhood, of course. To the

spirit I spoke about earlier. To what I felt like as a little girl. And I know now that I'm not alone; that I'm not the only one who's ever felt that way.

"That there were probably lots of other little girls and boys who were suffering the same sort of experience. And lots of grown men and women who, like me, are still carrying around the impact of their early childhood experiences.

"And so I see my experiences—the corralling of the wild horse, the stuffing away of the spirit my teachers and my parents trained me to do so well—as the beginning of a philosophy for my business, a philosophy that my business needs if I'm ever going to offer anything of true value to my employees and my customers.

" 'There will be no stuffing of the spirit here,' my business will say. Maybe I should put it up above the door to remind everyone who comes in what our purpose is." She grinned. "Or, maybe better yet, 'Let thy spirit run free!' Yes, that's better. It even feels better." She laughed aloud with the joy of it.

As she continued, it became so clear to me what a miraculous gift speaking can be.

I saw that Sarah wasn't so much talking to me but to herself, discovering as she spoke the miracles that lived within her, within her experience, within her relationship with her aunt, within her extraordinary imagination. Discovering truths she never knew she knew. Discovering all the wealth that was waiting there inside of her to be unearthed, to be explored, to be treasured as the words came tumbling forth.

As though the words, once freed by the speaking of them, combined with the air to become something else again. A vision. Understanding. Expansion.

Sarah continued.

"My picture of the business also goes back to what my aunt taught me about caring.

"If my aunt were alive today, she would say, 'If everyone cares, the pies will take care of themselves!'

"And so I can see my business as a school, a school about caring that teaches all the little things to my employees that my aunt tried so hard to teach me: What it means to pay attention. What it means—to our spirits!—to be present with the whole of ourselves in everything we do.

"My God, I thought I hadn't learned anything!" she said to me, her eyes wide with the astonishment of what she had just understood.

"But I had. I had. And now I'm going to take her place. That lovely woman. That sweet, gentle, determined, old woman. I'm going to take her place. I'm going to become the master in my own kitchen, just as she was the master in hers.

"And the rules of the game—what a joy it's going to be to create them. Rules about dress. Rules about comportment. Rules about the tools we use and how we use them. Rules about the floor and the walls and the counterspace, how we clean them every night and every morning, how we give them their final touch so that they absolutely glow! Rules about the pie tins and about the cupboards in which we store things. Rules about glass, rules about silver, rules about tin. Rules about the ovens, how they're heated, how they're opened and closed, how they're cleaned. Rules about opening up, and closing up. Rules about money, about keeping the books, about balancing at the end of each day. Rules about hair, about fingernails!"

Sarah's eyes were flashing as she poured out the beginning of her vision, as her vision began to take shape. She didn't need to know what the specific rules were yet; what was important was that she get a taste of the exercise.

As her aunt said, "The pies will take care of themselves."

Sarah was on her way.

"Talk to me more about management," Sarah said. "I heard you say earlier that I don't need professional managers to be successful in my business; that, in fact, I'm better off without them. What's wrong with hiring experienced managers?"

"Everything's wrong with it, Sarah!

"Because, if you don't know how to manage, how are you going to choose them, and how are you going to manage them?

"You can't!

"Because they will manage by the standards they have been taught to manage by in somebody else's business. Not by your standards.

"Remember Delegation rather than Abdication?

"You can't delegate your accountabilities, Sarah.

"Delegating your accountabilities is abdication.

"You, as the Shareholder, as the owner, as the COO, as the VP/Marketing, as the VP/Finance, whatever positions you take, must take full accountability for what's going on in your business.

"And to do so, you must lead the company in the direction you intend it to go.

"And that means you must set the standard.

"And one of the most important set of standards you must establish is a Management System through which all managers, and all those who would become managers in your company, are expected to produce results.

"Standards surrounding your Primary Aim. Your company's Strategic Objective. The rules of the game. The story you've been telling me about your aunt and about her extraordinary kitchen. And the standards that define the vision you hold in your heart, and in your head, for the business called All About Pies that you intend to realize!

"You don't need professional managers to manage to those standards. All you need are people who wish to learn how to manage to them. People who are as personally committed to those standards as you are!

"In short, you need people who want to play your game, Sarah. Not people who believe they have a better one.

"So, you need to invent the rules of the game, which become the foundation of your Management System.

"And once having created these rules, once having created this game, you need to invent the way to manage it.

"Because your managers don't simply manage people; your managers manage the System by which your business, All About Pies, achieves its objectives.

"The System produces the results; your people manage the system.

"And there is a Hierarchy of Systems in your business.

"This Hierarchy is composed of four distinct components:

"The first is, How We Do It Here.

"The second is, How We Recruit, Hire, and Train People to Do It Here.

"The Third is, How We Manage It Here.

"The Fourth is, How We Change It Here.

"And the 'It' I'm referring to is the stated purpose of your business. At Federal Express it's 'When You Absolutely, Positively Have to Get It There Overnight!'

"The 'It' of your business, Sarah, is Caring.

"How do you express Caring when you answer the telephone?

"How do you express Caring when you take a pie out of the oven?

"How do you express Caring when you take the money from a customer?

"And so forth and so on, in everything you do at All About Pies.

"And your answer to those questions is How You Do It Here! It is the sum total of everything you've created, every distinct process for performing every little task at All About Pies. Every bit of which is documented in your *Operations Manuals.* Every bit of which is taught at your school. Every bit of which is managed to, and improved upon, and discussed among you and your people for as long as you're in business! That's what 'It' is. 'It' is your Best Way. 'It' is what you believe in. 'It' is why people buy from you, work for you, lend to you, trust you.

"And just as in the hotel we've visited, it is the system, not only the people, that will differentiate your business from everyone else's.

"Imagine trying to produce such a consistent result without such a system!

"Imagine each manager in each of your future four stores doing his or her own thing.

"How would anything be communicated consistently in such a business, in which every form of language, every idea of organization, every kind of process and system were expressed in an individual and subjective way by each and every one of your people, without any standards, without any agreement, without any consistency in form—in fact, without any consistency in judgment?

"Is that an appealing picture?" I asked.

"I'm exhausted just thinking about it," Sarah responded.

"I know, and it is even worse than you can imagine.

"But a Management System is something else again. And when it is combined with a well-conceived Marketing System . . ."

17

YOUR MARKETING STRATEGY

What we have here is a failure to communicate.

Anonymous

Your Marketing Strategy starts, ends, lives, and dies with your customer.

So in the development of your Marketing Strategy, it is absolutely imperative that you forget about your dreams, forget about your visions, forget about your interests, forget about what you want—*forget about everything but your customer!*

When it comes to marketing, what you want is unimportant.

It's what your customer wants that matters.

And what your customer wants is probably significantly different from what you *think* he wants.

The Irrational Decision Maker

Try to visualize your customer.

He's standing before you.

He's not frowning; nor is he smiling. He is perfectly

neutral. Yet, there's something strange about him.

Coming out of his forehead, reaching up toward the ceiling, is an antenna! And at the end of the antenna is a sensor, beeping away like crazy.

And the sensor is taking in all of the sensory data around it—the colors, shapes, sounds, and smells of your store, or your office, or the restaurant where you're meeting for lunch.

The sensor is also taking in sensory data from you: how you are standing or sitting, the color of your hair, how your hair is combed, the expression on your face— Is it tense? Are you looking directly at him or off to the side?—the crease in your slacks, the color of your shoes—Are they shined? Are they worn? Are the laces tied?

Nothing escapes the sensor as it absorbs the stimuli from the environment.

Nothing escapes your customer as he absorbs the information he uses to make his decision to buy or not to buy.

But this step in the buying process is only the first.

It's what the sensor does with the information that's of interest here.

Because it's how the sensor processes the information that will determine the decision your customer is about to make.

Think of the sensor as your customer's Conscious Mind.

Its job is to gather the information needed for a decision.

Most of what it does, however, is unconscious; that is, automatic, habitual.

So even though your customer's Conscious Mind is

actively absorbing all manner and forms of impressions, it is totally unaware of most of them.

It can do it—literally—in its sleep.

In fact, it can't stop doing it!

Fortunately, the Conscious Mind doesn't need to be aware.

For it's not your customer's Conscious Mind that has to make the decisions.

It's your customer's Unconscious Mind.

It's in your customer's Unconscious Mind where all the action is.

It's in your customer's Unconscious Mind where the second step of the buying process takes place.

What is your customer's Unconscious Mind?

It's like a vast, dark, underground sea in which a multitude of exotic creatures swim about, single and in schools, silently seeking out food, each with entirely different needs and tastes.

Those creatures are your customer's expectations.

And the sea in which they swim is a truly foreign place to your customer.

He has no idea what's swimming around down there. What's lurking behind some subterranean rock. What's lying still and quiet as a stone on the bottom, waiting patiently and deliberately for some sweet morsel to wander by.

But you can rest assured that every creature in that sea—every one of those expectations—is a product of your customer's life!

Of his reactions, perceptions, attitudes, associations, beliefs, opinions, inferences, conclusions. An accumulation of all his experiences since the instant of his birth (and for all we know, before it) to this very moment when he stands before you.

And all his expectations are nothing more or less than the means through which the sum of them all—your customer's *personality*—gets fed what it needs.

The food it needs comes in the form of sensory input from the Conscious Mind (the "surface").

And if the food is compatible with its expectations, the Unconscious Mind says, "Yes."

And if the food is incompatible with its expectations, the Unconscious Mind says, "No."

And that decision, yes or no, is made at the instant it gets a taste!

In a television commercial, we're told, the sale is made or lost in the first three or four seconds.

In a print ad, tests have shown, 75 percent of the buying decisions are made at the headline alone.

In a sales presentation, data have shown us, the sale is made or lost in the first three minutes.

And all that happens after that psychographic moment of truth, after the buying decision is made, is that the Unconscious Mind sends its answer up to the Conscious Mind, which then goes back out into the world to assemble the rational armament it needs to support its already determined emotional commitment.

And that's how buying decisions are made.

Irrationally!

If anyone cared to do it, it could probably be proved that no one yet has ever made a rational decision to buy anything!

So when your customer says, "I want to think about it," don't you believe him.

He's not going to think about it.

He doesn't know how.

He's already done all the "thinking" he's going to do—he either wants it or not.

What your customer is really saying is one of two things: he is either emotionally incapable of saying no for fear of how you might react if he told you the truth, or you haven't provided him with the "food" his Unconscious Mind craves.

Either way, little or no thought enters into the transaction.

Despite what we would like to believe, the decision was made unconsciously and instantaneously.

In fact, it was made long before you ever met.

But your customer didn't know it.

The Two Pillars of a Successful Marketing Strategy

The question then becomes: If my customer doesn't know what he wants, how can I?

The answer is, you can't!

Not unless you know more about him than he does about himself.

Not unless you know his demographics and his psychographics.

Demographics and psychographics are the two essential pillars supporting a successful marketing program.

If you know *who* your customer is—demographics—you can then determine *why he buys*—psychographics.

And having done so, you can then begin to construct a Prototype to satisfy his unconscious needs, but *scientifically* rather than arbitrarily.

Again, demographics is the science of marketplace reality. It tells you who buys.

Psychographics is the science of *perceived* marketplace reality. It tells you why certain demographic types buy for one reason while other demographic types buy for another.

Let me give you an example of how these sciences might be utilized in your Marketing Strategy.

Notice the shade of blue on the jacket of this book. I call it "IBM Blue." Why? Because it's IBM's color. That's why, I imagine, IBM is called "Big Blue" in the marketplace.

Why that specific shade of blue rather than another? Why blue at all?

Because that shade of blue has an extraordinarily high appeal and preference to IBM's Central Demographic Model.

They see that shade of blue, and it's love at first sight!

Ever heard the expression, "True Blue"? That's what that particular color is: the color IBM's Central Demographic Model consumer knows it can depend on.

What do you think would have happened had IBM chosen orange instead of blue?

Well, since orange is at the opposite end of the preferential spectrum for IBM's consumer, the IBM success story may not have been so momentous. It's hard to imagine "Big Orange" instead of "Big Blue." I think IBM's customer would have had trouble buying an orange computer!

Now, I know that sounds ridiculous, but you can test it if you like.

Remember the little test I suggested earlier in this book, the one with the navy blue suit?

I'd like you to visualize someone wearing such a suit.

Can you see him in your mind's eye?

Deep navy blue, vents in the back, possibly a pin stripe. Sharply creased trousers. White starched shirt. A red and blue striped tie. Black, highly polished wing-tip shoes.

Now how do you feel about him?

Does he look businesslike?

Does he look like someone you can trust?

Does he appear to represent something solid, reliable, dependable?

Of course he does.

Research shows that the navy suit is perhaps the most powerful suit a person can wear in business. Instant impact.

Now visualize the very same person you did before, but this time he's not wearing a navy blue suit.

Now he's wearing an orange suit.

That's right, a two-piece orange suit!

An expensive one at that.

And with it, he's wearing a white-on-white silk shirt and a green and white striped Italian silk tie.

And a silver belt buckle with his initials in green jade across its face.

And a diamond tie pin, two carats, glimmering out at you just above the top button of his vest.

And proudly peeking out of his finely creased orange pants, an incomparable pair of white lizard cowboy boots!

Can you see it?

Do you get the picture?

Well, you better take it fast because he's out of business!

And what's important to know is that the difference between the two men isn't in them—it's in your mind.

Your Unconscious Mind.

What's more, the difference is perceived instantly without a moment of thought.

The fact that you couldn't conduct serious business

with the man in the orange suit but you could if he were wearing blue says that there is no such thing as reality. At least as we understand it.

Reality only exists in someone's perceptions, attitudes, beliefs, conclusions—whatever you wish to call those positions of the mind from which all expectations arise—and nowhere else.

So the famous dictum that says, "Find a need and fill it," is inaccurate.

It should say, "Find a perceived need and fill it."

Because if your customer doesn't perceive he needs something, he doesn't, even if he actually does.

Get it?

Those perceptions are at the heart of your customer's decision-making process.

And if you know his demographics, you can understand what those perceptions are, and then figure out what you must do to satisfy them and the expectations they produce.

You can know your customer's psychographic reality.

Each demographic model has a specific set of perceptions that are identifiable in advance.

Women of a certain age, with a certain amount of education, with a certain size family, living in a certain geography, buy for very specific psychographic reasons.

Those unconsciously held reasons will be different from another group of women, of a different age and marital status, with a different educational background, living in a different part of the country.

And these differences predetermine what each group buys.

Are you beginning to get a sense of the complexity of this business called marketing? I hope so.

Because until you do, until you begin to take it seriously, until you give it the earnest attention it demands, your Prototype will continue to be the only thing it could hope to be under the circumstances—a crap shoot!

At GERBER Business Development Corporation, we have created tools for our small business clients to begin the often arduous task of making demographic and psychographic determinations, and how to position their Prototype in the mind of their consumer. The impact has been astonishing.

Small businesses that acted like small businesses when we met them began to operate with intelligence.

Their customers came vividly alive to them, often for the very first time.

Inquiry, the active solicitation of specific information, and controlled experimentation replaced the guessing, blind hope, and feverish busy work that preceded them.

Innovation, Quantification, and Orchestration became the driving forces behind their efforts.

The fact is, any small business can do it. And every small business must!

If Mature businesses, such as IBM, McDonald's, Federal Express, and Disney, take such things seriously, then how can you not do the same?

Your business is far more fragile than a big business.

So if anything, you must take marketing more seriously than a big business does.

And time is running out.

We have entered the "unforgiving age."

An age in which countless small businesses will either accept the challenge of an information-glutted society or be destroyed by it.

An age in which your customer is deluged by so many products and promises that he becomes swamped in confusion and indecision.

The challenge of our age is to learn our customer's language. And then to speak that language clearly and well so that your voice can be heard above the din.

Because if your customer doesn't hear you, he'll pass you by.

No doubt you feel frustrated as you read this. You must be asking yourself: How do I do it? How do I determine my customer's demographics, his psychographics? What colors to use? What shapes? What words?

But if you're asking those questions, you're well on your way!

For the purpose of this book is not to answer those questions but to raise them!

Not "how to do it" but "what needs to be done."

Unless you understand what needs to be done, unless you understand the essential importance of marketing to your Prototype, unless you understand that your customer is far less rational in his convictions and expectations than you had ever imagined, unless you understand that your Prototype is your product—all the "how to do it" in the world won't make a bit of difference to you.

But we're not finished yet.

We have one more step to take in your Business Development Program.

Your Systems Strategy, the glue that holds your Prototype together.

"I know you don't want to talk about 'how to do it,' " Sarah said, squinting her eyes for mock emphasis, "but if you want to leave this table alive, you're going to have to give me more than that!"

"How do I determine the demographics and psychographics of my most important customer?" she implored me.

"Well," I began, "let's start where you are. What we already know about your business is that it's attracting someone to it. That the picture you have in your mind about the All About Pies you wish to create isn't that foreign from the one you've created. That while you didn't clearly formulate the ideas at the beginning of your business, we now know that your inner Entrepreneur was busy all the same. That the Caring you wish to express in the All About Pies of the future was in you all the time. It's expressed today in the delicious quality of your pies, the beauty of your shop, and, I might add, the lovely, albeit frazzled, state of your being."

She snorted quietly in response, and I went on.

"So, I believe it's safe for us to assume that the people coming in your door today are unconsciously expressing their preference for the Caring you have so eloquently shared with me. They're buying it even now!

"The first question you must ask, then, is: Who are they?

"Who are my customers, specifically? What is their Demographic Profile?

"How do you answer that question? You ask them!

"You ask each and every one of them, by having them complete a questionnaire in return for a free pie!

"The free pie is the price you pay for that information.

"The answers you get will prove to be a bonanza!

"But, while you're at it, you might as well get the

psychographic data you need, as well as the geographic data you need.

"How do you do that? You find out on your questionnaire what colors they prefer, what shapes, what words. You find out the brands of perfume they buy, automobiles, clothes, jewelry, food. You match those brands to the ads and commercials that sell them, and you discover by becoming interested in what messages are being sent to your customers by other companies—who are successfully selling to them—what messages you might send to those customers, who are demographically and psychographically the same as your existing Central Demographic Model, to intentionally come in your door.

"How do you find them, those people you have not yet met? You buy a list of those who fit your Central Demographic Model in what you've now determined to be your Trading Zone!

"What's your Trading Zone? It's the geographic perimeter within which your current customers mainly live. You take their addresses from your questionnaire, identify them on a map, draw a line around them, and that's your first-pass Trading Zone.

"You then buy a list of demographically correct people living in that area.

"Is that enough 'how to do it' for now?" I asked Sarah with mock impatience. "Will that keep you busy for a while?

"Because if it is, I'd like to go back to the 'what to do' for a minute. There's a lot more to it than meets the eye."

"This marketing thing isn't nearly as complicated as I might have made it seem," I continued. "But it's important that you take it seriously. Because it most often is regarded by small business owners as merely 'good common sense.' And I have seen more often than not that the only definition of 'good common sense' is 'my opinion.' That most small business owners, suffering as they do from what I've come to call 'willful disinformation,' simply decide what they want to do without any information at all, without any interest in what's true, and then simply do it. Stationery designed by the local quick-printer with a logo thrown in. Colors picked by their wives. Signs designed by the local sign guy whose experience is in painting signs, not in determining what colors and shapes are psychographically correct.

"In short, Sarah, while you don't have to go over the scientific deep end, you do have to be sensitive to the science of the marketing art. You have to be interested in it. In fact, you have to be interested in everything your business needs. You have to become a student of the art of business and the science of business. And that's the 'what to do' part of all this. Do you realize how much marketing money is spent by companies like McDonald's, Federal Express, Disney, and Walmart to get it just right? Do you realize how much time and attention companies like Pepsico and American Express spend to get their brands just right? And how easy it is to miss the mark? And what it costs them if they do?

"In a small business you simply can't afford to spend the money they do. But you can afford to spend the time, the thought, the attention, on the same questions they ask.

"And that's why I keep on going back to the true work of the small business owner—the strategic work rather than the tactical work. Because if you're doing tactical work all the time, if you're working all the time, devoting all your energy in your business, you won't have any time or energy left to ask, let alone answer, all of the absolutely critical questions you need to ask. You'll simply have no time or energy left to work *on* it.

"The owner of the business must start out by asking marketing questions.

"The COO must continue to ask marketing questions.

"The VP/Marketing is absolutely accountable for asking marketing questions.

"In fact, there isn't a function or position within the company that is free of asking marketing questions, if by marketing we mean, 'What must our business be in the mind of our customers in order for them to choose us over everyone else?'

"And so, seen from the appropriate perspective, the entire business process by which your company does what it does is a marketing process.

"It starts with the promise you make to attract them to your door.

"It continues with the sale you make once they get there.

"And it ends with the delivery of the promise before they leave your door.

"In some companies that process is called Lead Generation, Lead Conversion, Client Fulfillment.

"In your business, Sarah, it's called Marketing, Sales, and Operations.

"But whatever you call it, it is the essential key process that runs through every business.

"And it is how well-integrated that process is, how totally and completely connected each part of the process appears in relation to the rest of the process, that will determine how successful you are at getting them to come back for more.

"And it is getting them to come back for more that is the Primary Aim of every business.

"Because what McDonald's knows, and what Federal Express knows, and what Disney knows—indeed, what every extraordinary business knows—is that the customer you've got is one hell of a lot less expensive to sell to than the customer you don't have yet.

"And that's why the business process of Lead Generation, Lead Conversion, and Client Fulfillment is so critical to the growth of your business. And that's what marketing is. The whole process. Not just a part of it but the entire thing.

"And it never stops!

"And so, while the VP/Marketing and the VP/Operations and the VP/Finance each have their own specific accountabilities, they share one common purpose—to make a promise their customer wants to hear, and to deliver on that promise better than anyone else on the block!

"And the place where they join each other is at the position of COO. The COO is the driver of all this. The COO connects each part of the business process. The COO maintains the integrity of the whole by acting as the arbiter of the Strategic Objective he is accountable for fulfilling, of the rules of the game he is accountable for maintaining, of the game the business has chosen to play.

"And it is there, at that point in the middle, where Hierarchy and Process meet.

"It is there, at that point in the middle, that your business comes together.

"It is there, at that point where your Management System and your Business Development Process play out their respective roles so vividly.

"It is at that point, the point I have called the Power Point in an earlier book, that a business truly becomes alive.

"Where the static and dynamic nature of every great business meets. 'This is how we do it here,' and then, 'This is how we do it here,' and then, 'This is how we do it here,' over and over, and still over again.

"Continuous improvement.

"Electrifying, ecstatic, alive.

"To do what?

"To deliver the promise no one else in your industry dares to make!

"That's what marketing is, Sarah. That's what your business must be. Alive, growing, committed to keeping a promise no competitor would dare to make.

"That's what needs to be done. Are you ready to do it?"

"Just watch me," Sarah said.

"Then let's go on to the last part and tie it all together," I said.

"Let's take a look at Systems, and the absolutely essential role they play."

18

YOUR SYSTEMS STRATEGY

The world thus appears as a complicated tissue of events, in which connections of different kinds alternate or overlap or combine and thereby determine the texture of the whole.

Werner Heisenberg
Physics and Philosophy

Throughout this book I have talked about systems without really defining what a system is. So let me do that here.

A system is a set of things, actions, ideas, and information that interact with each other, and in so doing, alter other systems.

In short, *everything* is a system. The universe, the world, San Francisco Bay, the office I'm sitting in, the word processor I'm using, the cup of coffee I'm drinking, the relationship you and I are having—they're all systems.

Some systems we can understand and some we can't.

Let's take a look at the ones we can.

The systems in your business.

Three Kinds of Systems

There are three kinds of systems in your business: Hard Systems, Soft Systems, and Information Systems.

Hard Systems are inanimate, unliving things. My computer is a Hard System, as are the colors in this office's reception area.

Soft Systems are either animate—living—or ideas. You are a Soft System; so is the script for *Hamlet*.

Information Systems are those that provide us with information about the interaction between the other two. Inventory control, cash flow forecasting, and sales activity summary reports are all Information Systems.

The Innovation, Quantification, Orchestration, and *integration* of these three kinds of systems in your business is what your Business Development Program is all about.

What follows are examples of each, and how they integrate to produce a desirable result.

Hard Systems

At E-Myth Worldwide, we used to use "white boards" extensively in seminars, internal meetings, and conferences with clients and prospective clients. Since the vast majority of our work with clients is done by telephone, fax, and mail—rather than in our facilities as we did when *The E-Myth* was first published in 1986—we have few such meetings today.

As you've probably guessed by now, our facilities were operated (and, of course, still are) under rigid standards of color and cleanliness.

Color standards at the time dictated that we use *white* boards, rather than black ones, and blue markers, rather than white chalk. Unfortunately, our color standards also dictated that our walls be white.

It wasn't long before a conflict developed between our standards of cleanliness and our standards of color.

At the end of a seminar, a meeting, or a conference, the person accountable for that particular event was to leave the room in the order in which he found it. This included cleaning the board-work, which was not our employees' favorite job.

Not that they wouldn't do it; they would. But in their haste to get it done so they could get on with the work they preferred to do, the eraser would often fly uncontrollably over the edge of the board.

It wasn't long before our once gleaming white walls began to show ugly streaks and smudges of IBM-blue ink!

It drove us crazy.

We mounted an all-out campaign.

We held Blue Ink On the Walls Meetings.

We wrote memos entitled:

TO: *All Personnel.*
SUBJECT: *Blue Ink on Walls.*

We created new Board Cleaning Policies. We created Cleaning Teams. We created Wall Tours. We created Board Spot Checks. We installed signs above every board saying: BE CAREFUL!

But no matter what we did, no matter how hard we tried, no matter what we said to our normally meticulous people—blue ink got on the walls. Our only apparent recourse was to paint the walls white over and over again or go back to black boards and white chalk.

Neither was acceptable.

And that's how our Prevent-a-Smudge System was born.

We had one standard that insisted on impeccably clean walls and another standard that made the first one seemingly impossible to uphold (white boards, white walls, blue ink). In short, we had a conflict between what we wanted and what we had.

The two necessary components of conflict.

The essential conditions for innovation.

The conditions that give birth to a system.

But a third component was needed to translate the conflict we were experiencing into remedial action: *will*.

We were determined to lick the problem, and would not rest until we had.

Will applied to any conflict creates energy.

Conflict without will creates frustration. An engine turning, but going nowhere.

Conflict with will creates resolution, a movement beyond the dilemma.

Voilà! The E-Myth Worldwide Prevent-a-Smudge System!

It was so obvious. So simple.

We installed a clear Lucite collar around each board.

Extending four inches out from each edge of the board, the Lucite collar literally stopped the blue ink carnage in its tracks!

In one fell swoop, the walls were clean.

Our people were delighted; our clients amazed.

The constant painting, memo writing, sign creating, team invading, policy polluting activities that had pervaded our organization for more than three weeks were history.

And all because of a four-inch Lucite collar!

A Hard System for producing a human and totally integrated result.

A system solution to a typically people-intensive problem. Without anyone having to pay attention to it. Leaving me free to write this book, or anything else I cared to do.

After all, that's the purpose of a system—to free you to do the things you want to do.

Soft Systems

Things need to be sold.

And it's usually people who have to sell them.

Everyone in business has heard the old saw: 80 percent of our sales are produced by 20 percent of our people.

Unfortunately, few seem to know what the 20 percent are doing that the 80 percent aren't.

Well, let me tell you.

The 20 percent are using a system, and the 80 percent aren't.

A selling system is a Soft System.

And I've seen such systems produce 100 percent to 500 percent increases in sales in almost no time!

What is a selling system? It's a fully orchestrated interaction between you and your customer that follows six primary steps:

1. Identification of the specific Benchmarks—or consumer decision points—in your selling process.
2. The literal scripting of the words that will get you to each one successfully (yes, written down like the script for a play!).

3. The creation of the various materials to be used with each script.
4. The memorization of each Benchmark's script.
5. The delivery of each script by your salespeople in identical fashion.
6. Leaving your people to communicate more effectively, by articulating, watching, listening, hearing, acknowledging, understanding, and engaging each and every prospect as fully as he needs to be.

At E-Myth Worldwide, we call it the Power Point Selling System.

A career development company we worked with put it in the hands of people with no experience, and revenues increased 300 percent in one year.

An advertising agency put it in the hands of people with no experience in either selling or advertising, and revenues increased 500 percent in two years.

A health spa put it in the hands of people with no experience, and revenues increased 40 percent in two months.

If you put it to work in your company, it will do the same for you, no matter what kind of business you're in.

The Power Point Selling System is composed of two parts: Structure and Substance. Structure is *what* you do. Substance is *how* you do it.

The Structure of the System is all of the predetermined elements of the Process, and includes exactly what you say, the materials you use when you say it, and what you wear.

The Substance of the System is what you—the salesperson—bring to the Process, and includes how you say it, how you use it when you say it, and how you are when you say it.

Structure and Substance merge in the selling process to produce a far more extraordinary result than any single salesperson could if left to his own devices.

Let's look more specifically at the most important component of the Power Point Selling System—what you say. Or what we call at E-Myth Worldwide, the Power Point Selling Process.

THE POWER POINT SELLING PROCESS

The Power Point Selling Process is actually a series of scripts defining the entire interaction between the salesperson and the customer.

These scripts (or Benchmarks) are:

1. The Appointment Presentation
2. The Needs Analysis Presentation
3. The Solutions Presentation

THE APPOINTMENT PRESENTATION Most salespeople fail at the outset of the selling process because they don't realize the purpose of an Appointment Presentation.

Most believe that the purpose of an Appointment Presentation is to qualify the customer and ascertain whether or not he is a viable prospect. It's not.

The purpose of an Appointment Presentation is one thing and one thing only: *to make an appointment.*

The Appointment Presentation moves the prospect from where he is to the second Benchmark in the process, the Needs Analysis Presentation.

It is a series of words, delivered on the telephone or in person, that engage the prospect's unconscious (remember?) by speaking primarily about the product you have to sell rather than the commodity.

For example:

"Hi, Mr. Jackson. I'm Johnny Jones with Walter Mitty Company. Have you seen the remarkable new things that are being done to control money these days?"

"What new things?"

"Well, that's exactly why I called. May I have a moment of your time?"

The product? Financial control. Control is the key. The presentation tells Mr. Jackson that there are things going on in the world—"remarkable new things"—that he doesn't know about (he's out of control), but he can now become familiar with them (gain control!) by just spending a few moments with Johnny Jones.

And it tells him that instantly! Mr. Jackson's emotional commitment is already made. All that he needs now is to find the rational armament to support it. That's what Johnny Jones's job is. That's why the appointment will be made.

Simple and effective. It makes appointments.

To do what?

To deliver the Needs Analysis Presentation.

THE NEEDS ANALYSIS PRESENTATION The first thing you do in a Needs Analysis Presentation is repeat what you said in the Appointment Presentation to reestablish the emotional commitment:

> *"Remember, Mr. Jackson, when we first talked I mentioned that some remarkable new things were going on in the world to control money?"*

The second thing you do is tell the prospect how you would like to proceed to fulfill your promise to him:

> *"Well, what I'd like to do is to tell you about those things. At the same time, I'd like to show you some incredibly effective ways my firm, Walter Mitty Company, has developed to help you to control money here in your business. Okay?"*

The third thing you do is to establish your credibility in the prospect's mind by communicating two things. First, your company's expertise is such matters: "We are Money-Controlling Specialists" (we, at E-Myth Worldwide, call that a Positioning Statement). And second, your personal willingness to do whatever is necessary to utilize that expertise on his behalf:

> *"Let me tell you why we created our company, Mr. Jackson. We've found that people like yourself are continually frustrated by not being able to get the most out of their money. Frustrated by paying higher interest rates than they have to. By working with financial experts who don't seem to know what they're doing. By banking with a bank that doesn't seem to have their best interest at heart." And so on.*
>
> *"Do these things ever frustrate you, Mr Jackson? Of course they do And that's why Walter Mitty Company has created a Money-Controlling System that makes it possible for you to get the most preferential treatment in the finan-*

cial arena while paying the least for it. Now I know that
sounds too good to be true. But let me explain how we pro-
pose to go about doing that for you. . . . "

Here Johnny Jones is communicating that he understands what frustrates Mr. Jackson, and that he has the
expertise to alleviate those frustrations—not personally
but systematically—through the use of the Walter
Mitty Company's Money-Controlling System.

The fourth thing you do in a Needs Analysis Presentation is describe the Walter Mitty Company's Money-
Controlling System and why it works so well. Not what
it does but the impact it will have on the prospect:

"The Walter Mitty Company's Money-Controlling System
is designed to do three things, Mr. Jackson.

"First, it enables us to know what specifically bothers
you about controlling your money. Because we know that
controlling money must be personally tailored to each and
every one of our clients. In order to do that we've created
what we call at Walter Mitty Company a Money Manage-
ment Questionnaire. By asking you these particular ques-
tions, we're well on our way to helping you get what you
want. Before I leave today, I'll review the Questionnaire
with you.

"Once the Questionnaire is completed, we return it to
our Financial Systems Group. This is a group of financial
specialists who review your Questionnaire to make certain
that it has been completed accurately.

"If it has, they enter the information into our Money-
Controlling System that has been designed to analyze this
information and compare it with the broad spectrum of
data we've assembled over the years. Once having ana-

*lyzed the information, the System will then create person-
ally tailored solutions just for you, Mr. Jackson. Ways to
secure the kind of preferential treatment we talked about
earlier, but at the lowest possible cost. Ways of controlling
your money and using it to your advantage, not someone
else's.*

*"These solutions will then be prepared in the form of a
Financial Report that I'll deliver to you personally and
review with you at that time.*

*"Should any of our solutions make sense to you, we'll
be more than happy to help you implement them. If not,
then at least we'll have started the process of becoming
better acquainted so that we may be of assistance to you
some other time.*

*"In any case, the Financial Report is yours—at abso-
lutely no cost whatsoever. It's our way of saying we're serious about what we do, and would be happy to work with
you, whether now or in the future.*

*"So let's review the Questionnaire together, and when
we're done I'll provide you with a summary of some of the
remarkable new things that are happening in the world to
control money. And then I'll take your information back so
we can prepare your Financial Report. Okay?"*

The fifth thing Johnny Jones does in the Needs Analysis Presentation is complete the Money Management
Questionnaire.

The sixth thing Johnny Jones does is provide the
prospective customer with the information he promised
and show him how relevant it is to the Financial Report
he will be preparing for him. (He could have done this
at the outset of their meeting, during the Needs Analysis questioning process, or now, at the end.)

The seventh thing Johnny Jones does in the Needs Analysis Presentation is make an appointment with the prospective customer to return with the Financial Report, reminding him that Johnny Jones will have some valuable solutions for him—at no cost!—and that Johnny will take whatever time is necessary to help the prospective customer understand those solutions, whether he decides to implement them or not!

Upon completion of the Needs Analysis Presentation, Johnny Jones will have made an appointment that will bring him to the third Benchmark in the Power Point Selling Process, the Solutions Presentation.

THE SOLUTIONS PRESENTATION The Solutions Presentation is the easiest component of the Power Point Selling Process. Because if Johnny Jones has done his job effectively up to this point, the sale is already made.

Most salespeople think that selling is "closing." It isn't. Selling is *opening*. That's what the Needs Analysis Presentation does. It opens up the prospective customer to a deeper experience of his frustration and to the opportunities available to him by going through the questioning process with you.

You now have something to give him.

"Remarkable new things" that will make it possible for him to receive "preferential treatment" in the "financial arena" so as to secure the kind of "control" over his money he "deserves" and at a "preferentially" low cost.

In other words, by knowing you (or Johnny Jones), your prospective customer is going to: (1) be on the inside of the financial winners circle with people who are in the know; (2) be treated like important people are; (3) use money like the "pros" do; and (4) gain control over his life.

And he's going to get all of this without paying too high a price for it!

What more could anyone ask for?

The Solutions Presentation simply provides the rational armament for the emotional commitment (remember that?).

Here Johnny Jones brings the prospect up-to-date by reviewing everything he said and did during the Needs Analysis Presentation. The prospect has forgotten all those psychographically compelling things by now. But he won't for long—*they're a part of him.*

Then Johnny Jones reviews in great, patient, and earnest detail every last word, comma, and number in his prospective customer's Financial Report!

He asks questions to make certain that the prospect feels that this is his Financial Report, not Walter Mitty Company's.

And when Johnny Jones is done, when he's reviewed all of the components of the Financial Report prepared just for his prospect, Mr. Jackson, he asks him this question: "Of the options we've suggested here, Mr. Jackson, which do you feel would best serve you right now?" And then waits for the answer! Because the next person who speaks is going to make a purchase. If that's Johnny Jones, he's going to buy a "no sale."

And that's all, except for writing up the sale!

Of course, there's everything else to do.

What happens when the prospect says this?

What happens when the prospect asks me that? And so forth.

But believe me, whether you're selling sheets and

pillow cases, computers, swimming pools, flowers and fertilizer, canaries, puppies, or Quonset huts, the Power Point Selling Process will work.

How do I know that?

Because it already has!

But if the Process is to work for *you*, you must be willing to go through it the same way every single time. Using the same words the same way every time. Reviewing the Financial Report the same way every time.

And by doing it the same way every single time, you will not have a selling *person* but a selling *system*.

A Soft System.

A completely predictable technology for producing formerly unpredictable results.

And you will be able to tell just how predictable it is through the use of an Information System.

Information Systems

For an Information System to interact with the Soft System in our example, it should provide you with the following information:

INFORMATION	BENCHMARK
How many calls were made?	1
How many prospects were reached?	2
How many appointments were scheduled?	3
How many appointments were confirmed?	4
How many appointments were held?	5
How many Needs Analysis Presentations were scheduled?	6
How many Needs Analyses were confirmed?	7

How many Needs Analyses were completed?	8
How many Solutions Presentations were *scheduled?*	9
How many Solutions Presentations were *confirmed?*	10
How many Solutions Presentations were *completed?*	11
How many solutions were sold?	12
What was the average dollar value?	13

The information should be recorded on a form, either manually or as a database on your computer.

The Information System will track the activity of your Selling System from Benchmark to Benchmark.

It will tell you an astonishing number of things.

It could tell you the rate of conversion between any two Benchmarks in your Selling Process.

It could tell you at which Benchmark any particular salesperson needs help. Which of your people are "on the system"—that is, using the Selling System verbatim—and which ones are off it.

If you had calculated the cost of making a call, you could then calculate the cost of completing the next Benchmark in the process, and from that derive the next, and so on, until you calculate the actual cost of making one sale.

In short, the Information System could tell you the things you need to know!

Things you don't know now.

Things you need to know in order to develop, control, and change your Selling System.

And things you also need to know in Finance and Production and Product Development.

If your Systems Strategy is the glue that holds your Franchise Prototype together, then information is the glue that holds your Systems Strategy together.

It tells you when and why you need to change.

Without it, you might as well put on a blindfold, have someone turn you around three times, and set out with a dart in your hand, waiting for a signal from the heavens to throw it.

Not a very promising game.

But one, it seems, most people in small business are determined to play.

Hard Systems, Soft Systems, Information Systems.

Things, actions, ideas, information.

The stuff of which our lives are made, and the stuff of your business as well.

Do you see how difficult it is to separate one from the other?

Do you see how intertwined they are?

Do you now understand what I mean by your business system?

And why it is absolutely essential that you begin to think of your business as a fully integrated system?

That to approach any part of your business as though it were separate from all the rest would be lunacy, because everything in your business affects everything else in your business.

That your Primary Aim and your Strategic Objective and your Organizational Strategy and your Management Strategy and your People Strategy and your Marketing Strategy and your Systems Strategy—all of them are totally *interdependent*, rather than independent of one another.

That the success of your Business Development Program totally depends on your appreciation of that integration. And that your Prototype is that integration.

If you understand all of that, then this book has been worth our time.

If you don't, take off the blindfold, because there's no going around one more time.

We've got business to attend to.

There's no time left to trust a dart in the dark.

We were almost done. Sarah knew it and I knew it. All that was left was to tie the pieces together. To help her to integrate everything we had talked about together. To help her to see how it was all applicable—indeed, essential, to her business All About Pies.

"I understand what you mean by Hard Systems," she said. "The sign on my shop, the floors, the walls, the display cases, the tables, my people's uniforms, and so forth. In other words, all of the visual elements of my business and the way they all fit together. In fact, when it's all done correctly, the entire business should look like one fully integrated, beautifully designed system.

"I even understand what you mean by Information Systems," she continued. "My ability to extract from the day-to-day operation of my shops (she was already thinking about four shops, rather than one!), how many pies are sold, what kind of pies, the time they were sold, how many customers came in each shop and when, how many bought pies to go, how many slices of pie were sold to eat on the premises, how many of the customers who bought pie to eat on the premises bought a pie to go, and so forth. And I can imagine a good deal more than that I would like to know now that I've begun to think about it.

"What I don't fully understand is the Soft Systems part. Can you tell me a little bit more about that? I can't possibly imagine my people using—what did you call it? The Power Point Selling System?"

"I suspect you do without realizing it," I said.

"Remember what I talked about early on when we were discussing Innovation? 'Hi, have you been in here before?' as opposed to 'Hi, can I help you?'

"Well, what's your version of that?"

"Remember when we talked about the *Game Worth Playing* and the recruitment process the Manager used at the hotel?

"What about the script he used when he told the story about the Boss's game? What's your version of that?

"And remember when we talked about the hotel's checklists, and then went on to describe the Management System that defined them? What's your version of that?

"In fact," I continued, "every written or verbal communication with anyone who comes into contact with your business is a Soft System. What so few of us understand is the power of those words when they are totally integrated. That your recruitment script, and your shop's name, and the training you conduct in your school, and the words in your customer brochures, and your ads, everything you say, must work together just as the visual components of your shop must work together, to make one powerfully effective message.

"That you are All About Pies, and that there is no one, absolutely no one else like you.

"There is no one else telling the same story.

"There is no one else using these same words in exactly the same way as you are.

"And that these words represent the Idea behind All About Pies.

"The Idea that comes from your mind and your mind alone.

"The Idea that your aunt understood so well and that you understand so well.

"The Idea of your business, which is the lifeblood of your business. Which is the heart of your business. Which is the spirit of your business.

"And you know now how valuable that spirit is, Sarah. It's to be cherished. It's to be shared with others. It's to be set free upon the world.

"That's what Soft Systems are. Do you get it now? Do you see how all of this fits together into one lovely, endurable, however ever-changing, wonderful whole?

"Can you see now why I say that The Technician's role is not enough by far? That there's so much more to be done if your business is ever to live up to its potential?

"And that it's fun!"

Sarah was grinning from ear to ear.

For more information, visit us at www.e-myth.com.

19

A LETTER TO SARAH

Freedom does not come automatically; it is achieved. And it is not gained in a single bound; it must be achieved each day.

Rollo May
Man's Search for Himself

Dear Sarah,
It has been said that there are no accidents in the universe, and so I might consider it to be providential that on this very day that I'm writing this letter to you, I have just finished reading, for the third time, Rollo May's remarkable book, *Man's Search for Himself*. What a lesson that book holds for all of us in business who would believe that today's hot subjects of core values, meaning, purpose, and empowerment are advanced thinking when, in fact, Rollo May spoke more eloquently about those very same subjects in 1953!

For that matter, who among us today in business recalls May's Age of Anxiety, or Camus, or Dostoyevsky, or Kierkegaard, or Kafka, or Orwell, or T. S. Eliot in *The Hollow Men*, or David Riesman in *The Lonely Crowd*? To them, however, the question was not one of success in business but of life and death!

If we had such a yearning for values in 1953 when May's book was first published, and we have such a yearning for values today, what has happened to us in the interim? The Cold War? A trip to the moon? Korea? The Vietnam War? Cambodia? The Sexual Revolution? The Feminist Revolution? The Civil Rights Explosion? The Psychological Revolution? The New Age manifesto and the coming millennium? One hell of a lot I would say! And yet, after all that, and forty years, we are still searching for meaning, for something to believe in, and speaking about it as though it were brand new!

What lessons haven't we learned here at the end of the twentieth century, Sarah? Maybe we just don't care enough. Meaning, it seems to me, is the product of caring, not vice versa. What we care about we value. And so, as I look around, I see that we are in some very fundamental way disconnected from caring sufficiently to be able to find true meaning in the things that we do.

Which is not to say that we don't care about anything; we obviously do. We care about making money. We care about being safe. We care about being protected. We care about the Superbowl.

But I think that the things we have come to care about are insignificant when placed on the scale that Dostoyevsky, or Camus, or Tolstoy, or Kierkegaard, or Kafka, or the Old Testament, or the New Testament, or Rollo May would use. The problem is, Sarah, we're just not very serious people these days. We even speak about values, when we speak about them, as though they were a commodity like a sweater or a pair of Gucci pumps that can be acquired by writing a check. Much like the Leadership, Empowerment, Management, Relationship, and Quality Training seminars that abound today. As though by getting a little training we will suddenly find ourselves full of more substantial stuff. I think not, Sarah.

I think that we, playing our end game at the bottom of the twentieth century, are going to need one hell of a lot more than anything our "trainers" have in store for us. I think we need a shock, a self-administered shock, so jolting, so outrageous, so unsympathetic to our little wants, that we'll either be blown off the planet we've each shaped for ourselves—our personal little spaces— when we least expect it, or we will burn to a crisp right there on the spot, never to be heard from again.

And therein lies the problem, Sarah, and, of course, the opportunity. How does one come to the point in his or her life when he or she is not only ready but eager and willing—however terrifying the prospect might be—to self-execute such a leap of faith without any guarantees that it will do any good?

That, dear Sarah, is where I believe we left each other not too long ago, at a crossroads, where I stood and watched you walk off on your newly discovered path, thinking to myself that I knew where you were going and what you would discover there, and, at the same time, realizing I knew nothing of the sort. That the path you had chosen reached both forward in time and back to your childhood and the "spirit" you had thought you lost.

But what I know to be true from my own life experience is that you will not truly rediscover your "spirit" in the past but will discover it is waiting for you in the future on the path you have now chosen. Your spirit isn't behind you—it is way ahead of you; it has already made its choice! All that needed to happen was for you to make yours, and you were together again! Pretty mctaphysical for a hard-headed guy like me, perhaps, but while I can't prove it, I know without a shadow of a doubt that it is true.

I know, because the very same thing has happened to me, time and time again, when I was open to it. I know that my spirit is waiting out there in front of me on one of any number of a thousand paths, and that it's up to me to choose that one path on which my spirit waits, and to step out on it brightly, without hesitation, to pursue the *I*, which is the greatest one I can possibly be. To be spirit-full, that is, spiritual. That is to be in touch with my soul.

And there, in our spirit, Sarah, is where meaning lies. There, in what your aunt called caring. It is your spirit that cares, Sarah. While your parents and teachers thought it was disruptive and tried to take it away from you, your aunt knew, Sarah, what you've just found out. That your spirit was waiting there all the time! It hadn't gone anywhere; you had. And the path you are now on is the same path you and your aunt were on, there in the kitchen, and there in your little girl's bed on the summer morning as you breathed in the rich, delicate summer air, and there among the four oaks, and there with your hand on the face of the black horse.

Your path has always been there for you, Sarah. You simply got lost. You didn't trust it. In your need to be assured, as any little girl would, that your parents wouldn't leave you and that your teachers would love you, you became disconnected from yourself. But, fortunately, not forever.

Because this path you're now on, this entrepreneurial

path, winds around corners that will amaze you at times, and even shock you at others. To be sure, it will be anything but certain, but that's why it is so exciting! It's the path of surprise. It's the path of constant engagement. And because it's all those things, it is truly the path of life, or, as Rollo May might have called it, "the path of freedom." He said: "Thus freedom is not just the matter of saying 'Yes' or 'No' to a specific decision: it is the power to mold and create ourselves. Freedom is the capacity, to use Nietzsche's phrase, 'to become what we truly are.' "[1]

And so, Sarah, while we have talked a great deal about your business and its relationship to you, while we have spoken about planning and systems and controls and management, about people development and organizational development and marketing development, and all those many parts of your business you must become not only aware of but attentive to, I would be remiss if I left you with the impression that any of those things will make any difference at all unless you remember one thing: *keep the curtain up.*

The curtain is your Comfort Zone. And your Comfort Zone has been the false mask you put on when you were a little girl, because it was safe when your spirit was not. Your Comfort Zone has been the curtain you have placed in front of your face and through which you view the world. Your Comfort Zone has been the tight little cozy planet on which you have lived, knowing all the places to hide because it's so small. Your Comfort Zone has seized you before, Sarah, and it can seize you again, when you're least prepared for it, because it

[1]Rollo May, *Man's Search for Himself* (W. W. Norton & Company, Inc., 1953), p. 165.

knows what it means to you. Because it knows how much you want to be comfortable. Because it knows what price you are willing to pay for the comfort of being in control. The ultimate price, your life.

So, Sarah, if this new path, if living with your spirit, means anything to you at all, if you truly care about it, then guard it with your life. Because Comfort overtakes us all when we're least prepared for it. Comfort makes cowards of us all.

And so, good-bye for now. Please let me know how you're doing; how the business is going. And remember, my heart will be with you wherever you are.

BRINGING THE DREAM BACK TO AMERICAN SMALL BUSINESS

You should know now that a man of knowledge lives by acting, not by thinking about acting, nor by thinking about what he will think when he has finished acting. A man of knowledge chooses a path with heart and follows it.

Carlos Castaneda
A Separate Reality

This book is not simply a prescription for success; *it's a call to arms.*

But this call to arms is not a call to do battle. It's a call to learning.

How to feel, think, and act differently and more productively, more *humanly* than our existing skills and understanding allow. Today's world is a difficult place. Humankind has experienced more change in the past twenty years than it has in the 2,000 that preceded them.

Boundaries that once served us—geographically, politically, socially, emotionally—no longer exist. The rules are constantly changing. But people cannot live without boundaries, without structure, without rules.

So new ones have sprung up and proliferated in order to fill the void left by those that no longer seem to serve our "New Age" condition.

Unfortunately, in a world of accelerated change there is little time for rules to take hold. As soon as the new rules are upon us, they too are swallowed up in the insatiable vortex of change, followed all too quickly by more rules, and then still more.

The result of all this change is chaos and disorder, each change bringing with it an even more turbulent world than the one before it with fewer and fewer traditions to hold on to. A world in trouble, where confusion reigns.

But the trouble didn't start "out there" in the world. If it did, we'd really be in trouble. Because who among us knows enough to control or even have an impact on what's happening "out there"? If it is so difficult for us to do anything about our businesses, how in the world are we going to do anything about the world?

We can't. It's that simple. And any call to arms that suggests we can is a stopgap measure, a call to disillusionment and ultimately to disaster. Because our stopgap measures are not solutions. Our feeble attempts to fix the world can't change the overall condition. If they work at all, they can only change the circumstances in which we find ourselves at any given moment.

No, we can't change the world "out there." And fortunately, we don't have to; we can begin much closer to home. We can begin "in here." In fact, if we're to succeed, we must. Because the chaos isn't "out there" in everyone else. It's not "out there" in the world. The chaos is "in here" in you and me.

The world's not the problem; you and I are.

The world's not in chaos; we are.

The world's apparent chaos is only a reflection of our own inner turmoil.

If the world reflects a lack of good sense, it's because each one of us reflects the same. If the world acts as if it doesn't know what it's doing, it's because each one of us acts the same. If the world is violent, and greedy, and heartless, and inhuman, and often just plain stupid, it is because you and I are that way.

So if the world is going to be changed, we must first change our lives!

Unfortunately, we haven't been taught to think that way. We are an "out there" society, accustomed to thinking in terms of them against us. We want to fix the world so that we can remain the same. And for an "out there" society, coming "inside" is a problem.

But now is the time to learn how. Now is the time to change.

Because unless we do, the chaos will remain.

And we can't afford this kind of chaos much longer.

We're simply running out of time.

Bridging the Gap

And that's what this book is really about. Bridging the gap.

Between the "outside" and the "inside."

Between the world "out there" and the world "in here."

And your small business can become that bridge. The bridge between you and the world. The bridge that can draw together the world "out there" and the world "in here" in such a way as to make both more human.

In such a way that makes both more productive. In such a way that makes both worlds work.

For like the Boss's hotel, your small business can become your dojo, your practice hall. Joe Hyams, in his book *Zen in the Martial Arts*, tells us what a dojo is:

> A dojo is a miniature cosmos where we make contact with ourselves—our fears, anxieties, reactions, and habits. It is an arena of confined conflict where we confront an opponent who is not an opponent but rather a partner engaged in helping us understand ourselves more fully. It is a place where we can learn a great deal in a short time about who we are and how we react in the world. The conflicts that take place inside the dojo help us handle conflicts that take place outside. The total concentration and discipline required to study martial arts carries over to daily life. The activity in the dojo calls on us to constantly attempt new things, so it is also a source of learning—in Zen terminology, a source of self-enlightenment.[1]

And that is exactly what a small business is!

A small business is a place that responds instantly to any action we take. A place where we can practice implementing ideas in a way that changes lives. A place where we can begin to test all of the assumptions we have about ourselves. It is a place where questions are at least as important as answers, if not more so. It is a place where generalizations must give way to specifics. It is a place that demands our attention. A place where rules must be followed and order preserved. A place that is practical, not idealistic. But a place where ideal-

[1] Joe Hyams, *Zen in the Martial Arts* (Los Angeles: J. P. Tarcher, Inc., 1979), p. 12.

ism must be present for the practical to serve. It is a place where the world is reduced to manageable size. Small enough to be responsive, but big enough to test everything we have. A true practice hall.

A world of our own.

A World of Our Own

And that after all is the "Dream of American Small Business," the dream that has served as the catalyst for so many entrepreneurial—and not so entrepreneurial—efforts.

To create a world of our own.

What is this Entrepreneurial Revolution people are talking about today, where millions of us are going into business for ourselves?

It's nothing more than a flight from the world of chaos "out there" into a world of our own.

It's a yearning for structure, for form, for control. And for something else as well. Something more personal. Something less distinct, yet much more intimately connected with who we are as human beings. It's a yearning for relationship with ourselves and the world in a way impossible to experience in a job.

Unfortunately, as we've already seen, the "dream" is rarely realized; most small businesses fail. And the reason is obvious. *We bring our chaos with us.*

We don't change. We try to change "out there." We try to change the world by starting a small business—but we stay the same!

And so the small business that was started to give us a new world becomes instead the worst job in the world!

The lesson to learn from all this is simple: *we can't change our lives by starting "out there."* All we can produce in the process is more chaos!

We can only change our lives and create a world of our own if we first understand how such a world is constructed, how it works, and the rules of the game. And that means we have to study the world and how we are in it. And in order to do that we need a world small enough in scope and complexity to study.

A small business is just such a world.

And a Business Development Program can be a means to study it most effectively.

And the Franchise Prototype can provide our study with the discipline it needs to succeed.

Innovation, Quantification, and Orchestration become the practice that brings us and our opponent—whoever that may be—to the discovery of our limits, our weaknesses, our strengths. To the discovery of what really works in the world rather than what our imaginations might wish would work. For in a martial arts contest, there is no room for imagination. We could get killed out there!

Innovation, Quantification, and Orchestration provide the belief system of our business, the philosophical bedrock of our interaction with the world. They become our source for learning, for creating, for expanding beyond our self-imposed limits.

And through Innovation, Quantification, and Orchestration our business can become something more than merely a place to go to work. It can become a place that satisfies more of ourselves than just The Technician. There is a place in Business Development for the whole of ourselves. For the innovator, for the maintainer, for the doer. For The Entrepreneur, The Manager, and The Technician in each one of us.

Your small business and mine can give us more life.

An Idea for Action

But does it work?

Will the model of the Franchise Prototype work for you?

There is an old Chinese proverb that says:

When you hear something, you will forget it.
When you see something, you will remember it.
But not until you do something, will you understand it.

In short, my answer is a resounding, "Yes!" It does work. Every time it's applied. And it will work for you. It works because it requires the full engagement of the people working it. It can't be done half-heartedly. It can't be done frenetically. It can only be done intelligently, reasonably, intentionally, systematically, and compassionately.

The very Process of Business Development creates instantaneous change in the people who engage in it.

And that is the key to its success.

Those who engage in the process must remember their aim in order to continue it. And in the process of remembering, their aim becomes tethered to something real in the world—their business. A place in which aims can be tested in a concrete, practical way. The business becomes a symbol for the life they wish to live, a visible manifestation of who they are and what they believe. A living, active, evolving testament to the will of man.

But, I ask you not to think about it anymore.

It's time to act.

Because until you do, you won't understand it.

And when you do, there will be nothing left to think about—you'll be well on your way.

Until then, it's just another good idea, just another creative thought.

It's time to turn it into an innovation.

It's time to Bring the Dream Back to American Small Business.

It's been gone far too long.

Afterword
TAKING THE FIRST STEP

So now what do you do?
Now that the fire is burning. Now that you want to get started. Now that you want to turn your business into a little "money machine," a turn-key operation.

Well, like Sarah, and thousands of small business owners just like her, you must take the first step.

You must step back from your business and look at it through your new E-Myth eyes.

You must analyze your business as it is today, decide what it must look like when you've finally got it just like you want it, and then determine the gap between where you are and where you need to be in order to make your dream a reality.

That gap will tell you exactly what needs to be done to create the business of your dreams.

And what you'll discover when you look at your business through your E-Myth eyes is that the gap is *always* created by the absence of systems, the absence of a proprietary way of doing business that successfully differentiates your business from everyone else's.

Since *The E-Myth* first appeared in 1986, we at E-Myth Worldwide have assisted thousands of small-business owners in taking that first step back from their businesses to discover what the gap was in each of their cases.

We would love to do the same for you. It begins with our invitation to take part in our *free* E-Myth Experience™. You will learn how to cross the bridge from where you are to where you want to be in your business, your life, and your future. The E-Myth Experience will take you to a place you have never been before, and it will feel like home.

To take your first step, simply complete the form at the back of this book and follow the instructions provided.

And remember . . .

When you hear something, you forget it.
When you see something, you remember it.
But not until you do something will you understand it.

Let's get started.

Michael E. Gerber
E-Myth Worldwide
Santa Rosa, California
June, 2001

About the Author

MICHAEL E. GERBER is the Founder, Chairman and CEO of E-Myth Worldwide, the company he founded in 1977 to provide small-business owners and entrepreneurs with the help they need to build a business that works. Since then, E-Myth Worldwide has provided more than 25,000 small and emerging business-owner clients with the means to radically transform their businesses and their lives. It is fast becoming world-wide the largest and most effective small-business development resource of its kind.

Thought by many as "the leading voice of small-business in America," Michael Gerber has spoken to thousands of small-business owners, managers, and corporate executives throughout the world about the truly profound role the entrepreneurial perspective can play in the reinvention of the world's economy and culture. His message is unique, compelling, and pragmatic. And best of all, as his thousands of readers, business clients, and seminar participants attest, it works.

If you are interested in having Michael Gerber address your organization, or wish to receive more information about Mr. Gerber's innovative E-Myth Mastery Program, books, and tapes, call Toll Free: 800-221-0266 (US) or 707-569-5600 (worldwide). Or write to: Michael Gerber, E-Myth Worldwide, 131 Stony Circle, Suite 2000, Santa Rosa, California, 95401. Visit us at our Web site: www.e-myth.com or send us an email: info@e-myth.com.

BOOKS BY MICHAEL E. GERBER

THE E-MYTH PHYSICIAN
Why Most Medical Practices Don't Work and What to Do About It
ISBN 0-06-093840-4 (paperback)
Gerber shares powerful insights that will lead independent physicians to successful practices and enriched lives.

THE E-MYTH CONTRACTOR
Why Most Contractors' Businesses Don't Work and What to Do About It
ISBN 0-06-093846-3 (paperback)
Gerber applies his E-Myth Revolution specifically to contractors—the largest group of clients Gerber serves.

E-MYTH MASTERY
The Seven Essential Disciplines for Building a World Class Company
ISBN 0-06-072318-1 (hardcover)
ISBN 0-06-075924-0 (audio CD)
Presenting practical exercises to help small business owners recover their vision and passion, Gerber clears a path for getting back to the basic disciplines for business success. *E-Myth Mastery* is the ultimate business development program that will help you recover your passion and turn your company into a world-class operation—a turn-key machine for the money and satisfaction that only a successful entrepreneur can enjoy. Get started today!

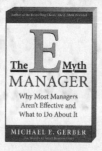

THE E-MYTH MANAGER
Why Most Managers Aren't Effective and What to Do About It
ISBN 0-88-730959-3 (paperback)
Drawing on lessons learned from working with more than 15,000 organizations, Gerber offers a fresh, provocative alternative to management as we know it.

THE E-MYTH REVISITED
Why Most Small Businesses Don't Work and What to Do About It
ISBN 0-694-51530-2 (audio)
ISBN 0-06-075559-8 (audio CD)

Don't miss the next book by your favorite author.
Sign up for AuthorTracker by visiting *www.AuthorTracker.com*.

Available wherever books are sold, or call 1-800-331-3761 to order.